THE NATIONAL MOVEMENT

Studies in Ideology and History

THE NATIONAL MOVEMENT

Studies in Ideology and History

IRFAN HABIB

Tulika Books

Published by

Tulika Books
35 A/1 Shahpur Jat, New Delhi 110 049, India

© Safdar Hashmi Memorial Trust, 2011

First edition 2011

Second edition 2013

ISBN: 978-81-89487-79-9

Printed at Chaman Enterprises, Delhi 110 006

Contents

Preface

It is now sixty-four years since India gained Independence, and so personal memories of British rule and the National Movement that arose to overthrow it have naturally dimmed. And yet those who participated in it had visions of what India would be, when its people became masters of their destiny; and these visions can never lose their topicality. In the five essays here presented three are devoted to the two men, Mahatma Gandhi and Jawaharlal Nehru, whose divergent ideas dominated the National Movement and to different degrees influenced its course. One further essay studies in detail how ideas and practice enmeshed to produce the Civil Disobedience Movement in its initial phase, 1930–31, being undoubtedly the most powerful mass agitation organized by the Congress. The final essay studies the contributions made by the Left, especially the Communists, to the National Movement, seeking to fill a gap quite often found in conventional histories.

As footnotes on the opening page of each essay are provided particulars about the year and publication of the original text of each piece. I have taken the liberty of revising the previously published texts of all these essays, hoping thereby to impart greater clarity to the exposition. This does not apply to the third essay, 'Jawaharlal Nehru's Historical Vision', which is being published for the first time.

I am grateful to Rajendra Prasad for first suggesting and then undertaking the publication of this volume.

August 2011   IRFAN HABIB

1

Gandhiji: A Life

Mohandas Karamchand Gandhi was born on 2 October 1869 in the sleepy seaside town of Porbandar in Kathiawad, Gujarat. His family of Modh Banias had apparently little commercial interests, its members mainly nursing the ambition of serving as 'dewans' under any of the numerous princelings of Kathiawad. Gandhi's father, Kaba, rose to be the Dewan at Rajkot. He maintained traditional beliefs respecting the numerous customary taboos, including strict vegetarianism; and yet there were friendships with Jains, Parsis and Muslims at personal levels, characteristic of old society. The mother, Putlibai, was strict about vows and rituals. Except for a modern-style school education, Gandhi thus had a fairly conservative upbringing. He was not more than thirteen when he was married to Kasturba, an illiterate child, who was later so loyally to share her husband's travails.

Gandhi says in his frank autobiography that he was 'mediocre' at his studies, and the suggestion of a family friend that he should go to England to become a barrister was welcome to him since it freed him from the dull business of reading for his B.A. degree at the college at Bhavnagar. He overlooked the financial burdens his family would have to bear, now that his father was dead; he also disregarded the ban imposed on his departure by his caste-headman at Bombay. Gandhi sailed for England in 1888 and back for home, after having been called to the bar, in 1891. The encounter with Victorian England, with its freedom

This article was written for a SAHMAT publication, *Addressing Gandhi*, New Delhi, 1995.

of social intercourse and women's aspirations of equality, had a potentially greater role in the formation of Gandhi's personality and thought than is perhaps often recognized. On the one hand, while in England Gandhi tried to remain loyal to his traditional background, which for him took the form of a semi-fanatical belief in vegetarianism. On the other hand, he met through the vegetarian movement itself, earnest Christians as well as liberals, contacts that began to kindle in him a humanism which he tended to treat as the message of true religion. This last he looked for in the *Bhagvad Gita*, which in English translation he read now for the first time, along with the New Testament. It is possible that a genuinely nationalist sentiment also began to take root, for he attended every public speech delivered in London by Dadabhai Naoroji, quietly coming away 'having feasted my eyes and ears'.

On his return home, Gandhi realized that he was not cut for a grand career as a barrister in the manner of Sir Ferozshah Mehta. With his usual modesty, he attributed it later to his own lack of clear, logical articulation and capacity for oratory. In 1893 he sailed for South Africa to undertake a case for a Meman firm, Dada Abdulla & Co. It was in South Africa that Gandhi was destined to organize from scratch, a movement to obtain and defend elementary rights for the Indian settlers. Had this been his sole achievement it would have been remarkable enough, for it was a mobilization of the poor on modern lines, the like of which had not till then been seen even in India. But what set him really apart was an increasing anxiety to relate the day-to-day work and struggle to a larger vision for humanity, which he painfully groped for, step by step, as he experienced, read and reflected. Central to this endeavour, and the source of much heart-searching for him, was a unique insistence to practise what he had once decided to preach. Immediately on arrival in South Africa, Gandhi had personal experiences of colour prejudice from which England, with its imperial responsibilities to care for, had seemed, at least on the surface, largely immune. He was off-loaded from a train at an intermediate station for daring to travel first-class for which he held a ticket; and he was only a 'coolie-barrister', required to remove his turban in the court. 'I discovered', Gandhi was to recall later, 'that I had no rights as a man because I was an Indian.' It happened that Abdulla Sheth and his fellow Gujarati merchants (in the beginning mostly Muslim) not only gave him assistance in his personal difficulties, but encouraged him to take up the grievances of the Indian community.

The first political document by Gandhi was a defence of the 'Indian trader' in South Africa (September 1893). His first major action was to organize a mass petition against bills to deprive Indian settlers of their franchise in Natal (June 1894). This was preceded by the formation of the Natal Indian Congress (22 May), with Gandhi as its first Secretary. If the Natal Indian Congress derived its name from the Indian National Congress, it yet was a different kind of organization. The parent Indian organization was then a rough alliance of patriarchs who assembled with their followers once a year to deliver speeches, pass resolutions and disperse. Gandhi's Congress was a body of members ready to pay £3 a year, which meant a mercantile and middle-class membership, expecting constant activity – meetings, educational work, propaganda. This work speedily brought Gandhi in contact with the most oppressed and impoverished Indians, the indentured labourers. In 1894 he led an agitation against the poll-tax of £25 imposed on indentured Indians; as a result of the agitation it was reduced to £3 – undoubtedly the first success of any struggle on behalf of the indentured. Gandhi utilized a visit to India, in 1896–97, to meet the Indian political leaders and get them interested in the struggle of the Indians in South Africa. He had his first brush with racial violence when on his return to Durban in January 1897, he was nearly lynched by a white mob. Thereafter he busied himself organizing a campaign against the Natal bills restricting Indian immigration and imposing other disabilities on Indians. He thought that the Indian cause would be served well if the Indians helped the British in the Boer War (1899–1902). Having trained as a medical assistant himself, he led an ambulance corps which did much service for the injured. Gandhi was later similarly to organize a corps of stretcher-bearers in the Zulu rebellion (1906), although even at the time of the offer of assistance the Natal Indian Congress refused to commit itself to any opinion about 'the cause of the Native revolt', and Gandhi was later to say that their corps was the only one that tended wounded Zulus.

Gandhi's sojourn in India (1901–02) was cut short by a call from South Africa. The end of the Boer War began the process of the formation of a united white ruling class, the Boer–English merger being consummated in the Union of South Africa (1910). Colour-bar came to be the basic ideological principle of the new political formation. Gandhi began to respond to the increasing racist pressure by bringing out *Indian Opinion* in English and Gujarati as a weekly journal from 1904. Next came the crucial phase – that of resistance. In 1907 Gandhi led volunteers to court imprisonment against Transvaal's Asiatic Act, and called upon Indians not to register and fingerprint. This was first called Passive Resistance, and then Satyagraha ('firmness for truth'). The prisoners waived the privilege of their own clothing and wore the same dirty clothing as issued to the 'negro' convicts – a first hesitant step towards inter-racial solidarity. In January 1908 General C.A. Smuts agreed to a settlement and released the prisoners. Smuts's betrayal of the settlement and passage of harsher measures led to an immediate revival of agitation, with the burning of identity certificates in a bonfire, followed by Gandhi's mission to England (1909). But there was little success to be got from mere appeals, not even from Gokhale's visit and negotiations (1912). Even Indians' marriages began to be held invalid by South African courts (1913). Gandhi's last struggle (the greatest of all) in South Africa included a defiant Satyagraha by women, whom the regime put in prison for three months (October 1913). Then came the legendary march of the Indian indentured mine workers, over 2,000 of them with over 50 women, who first struck work and then assembling, crossed into Transvaal, braving police and prison. Both actions were so unprecedented that Smuts at last capitulated. An Indians' Relief Act (1914) was passed, abolishing the £3 annual tax on Indian workers and validating Indian marriages. The success gave Gandhi an opportune moment to bid farewell to South Africa.

The twenty-one years that Gandhi spent in South Africa saw the formation of the principal elements of his thought. The general belief that these derived from his roots in the Indian tradition of *bhakti* and *ahimsa* has no basis in Gandhi's own autobiographical writings. The source was modern humanitarian and pacifist thought. This reached him, first, through the close contact (even some formal affiliation) that Gandhi established with European Christians, especially during the 1890s. This stressed the message of peace and conscience, which was conveyed most persuasively to Gandhi through his reading of

Tolstoy's 'Christian' writings during this period. In 1906 he read Ruskin's *Unto This Last*, drawing from it a recognition of the overriding necessity of welfare of all (*Sarvodaya*, the title of Gandhi's Gujarati translation of the book) and the value of manual labour. These ideas could be implemented in respect of his own person and select groups through 'settlements'. The Phoenix Settlement grew out of Gandhi's own home at Phoenix in Natal (1904), and the Tolstoy Farm, a communistically run economic unit near Johannesburg, was established later (1910). There was little in common between these and the religious ashrams of Indian tradition. The settlements were to be models where social equality beyond caste or race (with considerable participation by women) could be practised. Here too Gandhi could practise and propagate his personal 'fads', e.g., vegetarianism, other dietary controls, abstention from the conjugal side of marriage, etc. But he led the others in working with his own hands, and he had no compunction in handling dirt and waste. Gandhi's thought during this period displays a lack of concern (positive or negative) with socialism and a very simplistic view of anarchism. Non-violent struggle and compromise are usually tactical forms imposed on those working in either a democratic framework or where the opponent is very strong. Irish nationalism, as much as European trade unionism, created set forms of such struggle: strike, picketing, 'boycott', passive resistance, etc. These restraints were unavoidable in the struggle of a small minority like that of Indians in South Africa. But to Gandhi these became essential aspects of what was something even beyond long-term strategy, namely, a full-fledged faith in *ahimsa* and *sarvodaya*: peaceful means and mutual accommodation of all interests. The oppressed were to be roused, the oppressors to be persuaded. This outlook made it possible for Gandhi to enter the huts of the poor as no modern Indian leader had done till then; it also enabled him to have in South Africa such staunch European collaborators as the Polaks, Kallenbach, C.F. Andrews and others. It is, therefore, not a little strange that the black Africans should have remained so much outside his strategic vision as one can see from his own *Satyagraha in South Africa* (1925): they were people to be sympathized with, and that too in passing, but not seen even as potential allies of the Indian settlers. One cannot escape thinking that here, both a fear of the white onslaught and of loss of support from many Indians (themselves not free of racial bias) counted. Yet Gandhi left behind a legacy of struggle against the white rulers of South Africa, and the great African National Congress acknowledges by its very name that common legacy with India.

While aboard ship from England to South Africa in 1909, Gandhi wrote *Hind Swaraj* ('Home Rule for India') in Gujarati. This text, in the form of a dialogue between Gandhi as 'Editor' and a radical Indian nationalist as 'Reader', is an important statement of the set of ideas with which Gandhi began his work in India in 1915. *Hind Swaraj* begins with a defence of two nationalist spokesmen, whom Gandhi had been in touch with and who did much to support him – Dadabhai Naoroji and Gopal Krishna Gokhale. Both were modernizers and moderates. Gandhi went on to give an image of the Indian nation which they would have approved: nationality was not synonymous with religion, and so Hindus, Muslims, Parsis and Christians 'will have to live in unity'. In its initial part the work, then, states broadly the moderate nationalist point of view; but then comes about a dramatic turnaround. Swaraj is not to be 'English rule without the Englishman', not a modernized India ('you would make India English'); the India of the past has to be restored: an agricultural, non-industrialized India, though purged of its own evils and divisions. 'Swadeshi' must mean rejection of western machinery, not 'reproducing Manchester in India'. Before the English rule could be terminated, there had to be a long period of self-correction, for only 'if the cause of India's slavery [viz. its divisions, its imitation of the modern European civilization] be removed, India can be free'. The ordinary people of India, away from the towns, poor, but least tainted by modern civilization, were to be mobilized for 'passive resistance' by leaders 'who observe perfect chastity, adopt poverty', etc. We would then be in a position to 'cease to cooperate with our rulers when they displease us'.

Hind Swaraj is undoubtedly a text of heavy exaggeration, both in its criticism of western civilization and in its idealization of pre-British India (which Gandhi is always careful not to identify with a 'Hindu India'). On the other hand, India's own traditional evils, in a short list, are almost casually admitted. Untouchability, on which Gandhi had already felt so strongly that he was ready to break up his home over it, is not even mentioned here. One could even smile over Gandhi's reading-list of twenty items, of which eighteen came from European pens and the remaining two from Indian modernizers. Clearly, Gandhi's own picture of an ideal civilization had roots not in Indian, but in western thought. As may be expected, Gokhale in 1912 was dismayed to read the book, 'so crude and hastily conceived', and hoped for its withdrawal. In 1933 Gandhi himself recognized that he had 'discarded many ideas and learnt many new things' since writing *Hind Swaraj*, for truth, not consistency, was his object. Yet the book retains its importance as representing the starting-point of the ideological development of the mature Gandhi.

How far the real old India was from Gandhi's own idealization of it could have been borne upon him when he set about transferring his Phoenix Settlement to the Satyagraha Ashram that he established at Ahmedabad in 1915. The admission of an untouchable family – not by him, confessed Gandhi later, without perturbation – led to the cessation of donations, social boycott and internal tensions. Gandhi's response was to plan to shift to 'the Untouchables' quarter' in the city; and only an unexpected gift of money by an unidentified 'sheth' saved the ashram. This episode also brings into focus Gandhi's relationship with the Indian capitalist class. In *Hind Swaraj*, they, as industrialists, could have had no future, since industry was to be curtailed if not eliminated. Yet in the institutions of struggle that Gandhi was now fashioning, their assistance was most welcome; but with this assistance would undoubtedly come influence in the formulation of the day-to-day policies, if not the basic faith.

In spite of his condemnation of western civilization, Gandhi continued to retain the moderates' faith in the British empire: 'I had hoped', he later recalled, 'to improve my status and that of my people through the British empire.' While he was in England, to which he went first after leaving South Africa, World War I broke out, and he set out to organize an Indian ambulance corps for British troops (1914). He even conducted an army recruitment campaign in Gujarat as late as 1918. But if there was a sense of affiliation, if not loyalty, to Britain, this coexisted with his participation in efforts to develop a movement for Home Rule. He fully supported the rapprochement between the Congress and the Muslim League, which Tilak laboured for and achieved in the Lucknow Pact (1916). In *Hind Swaraj* Gandhi had made his position clear by his disapproval of the opposition of some Hindus to the concessions Muslim leaders had sought for their community from Lord Morley. Yet he was not at home in the higher politics of 'Home Rule', and felt that his primary duty was to go to the poor and take up their grievances, for which his life and work in South Africa had been the ideal preparation.

Gandhi began with his famous Champaran Satyagraha of 1917. Defying and overcoming an official ban, he toured this northern district of Bihar, collecting information on the oppressive conduct of the European indigo planters. The demands framed were moderate, but they undercut the planters' dominance of the countryside. When Edward Gait, the Governor of Bihar, through the usual enquiry commission, gave in to the demands, hundreds of thousands of peasants learnt for the first time that the masters were not invincible and could be opposed. On Gandhi's own part, it seemed as if in 'meeting with the peasants I was face to face with God ...'. Gandhi followed the Champaran struggle with the Kheda Satyagraha in 1918, though here the primary grievances were those of the upper peasants (*patidar*s) against the revenue authorities.

In between came Gandhi's experiment with a Satyagraha involving industrial workers. Here the opposing side was that of his own supporters, the Ahmedabad mill owners. When the mill workers' strike began to falter, Gandhi went on fast (15–18 March 1918) to force a settlement. It seems, however, that despite this first use of fast as a weapon, the Ahmedabad success had no important sequel in trade unionism; his anxiety not to hurt the Indian mill owners' interests unduly always inhibited any support to militant working-class action.

Gandhi turned next to what, to begin with, was the grievance of the educated middle classes, whose political activity was the avowed reason for the British Government to pass the Rowlatt Act (March 1919), giving itself powers to suppress all expression of unwelcome opinion and detain anyone without trial. The Act was passed in the teeth of a total Indian opposition in the Imperial Legislative Council. But it was left to Gandhi to organize an active opposition through a Satyagraha Sabha, which called for an all-India *hartal* on 6 April and for Civil Disobedience. The success of the *hartal* broadened the sweep of the movement; and the government answered with strong repressive measures, resulting in the Jallianwala Bagh massacre (13 April) and imposition of martial law in the Punjab. Perhaps staggered by the repression, Gandhi confessed to a 'Himalayan miscalculation' and withdrew Civil Disobedience (18 April). He, however, devoted himself to preparation of the Congress Report on the Punjab repression (March 1920), on the basis of which the rectification of the 'Punjab wrongs' was to remain a nationalist slogan for a long time. Characteristic of Gandhi's moderation at this time was his opposition still to the boycott of the 1919 Constitutional Reforms. At the Amritsar Congress (December 1919), it was his resolute intervention that prevented the Congress from taking a decision in favour of boycott of the elections under the Act of 1919.

It is, therefore, all the more startling to find Gandhi giving the call for Non-Cooperation in 1920, not on any Indian issues, but over Turkey and Khilafat. There is no doubt that this can be understood only in the world context. For the world had changed suddenly. On the one hand, the Allies' total success in World War I meant that British imperialism, with France as its junior ally, having disposed of the major rival Germany, was prepared to brook no opposition among subject peoples. On the other, the Soviet Revolution of 1917 and the successful defence of Soviet Russia against Allied intervention (1919), together with the banner of independence of Turkey raised by Mustafa Kamal, showed that resistance to imperialism was possible. It was the genius of Gandhi that enabled him to see in Khilafat the crucial factor in the situation. If the struggle for it was successful, it could throw British imperialism off balance in the world arena and thereby bring Swaraj so much nearer; in India, it could arouse in the Muslim masses an enthusiasm for the National Movement that the Lucknow concessions of 1916 on distribution of council seats had failed to elicit. Gandhi had already in 1918 demanded the release of the Ali brothers, and now (December 1919), as they and Abul Kalam Azad were freed, he joined with them and others to plan the Khilafat struggle. At Delhi, on 22 March 1920, in a joint meeting of Hindu and Muslim leaders, he proposed 'Non-Cooperation' as the means of defending and restoring the Khilafat. The idea spread; and Gandhi's new organs, *Young India* and *Navajivan* (Gujarati), helped to carry the message. On 1 August Non-Cooperation began over Khilafat and the rectification of the

Punjab wrongs. The special session of the Congress at Calcutta by majority vote, with many established leaders opposing, voted in September 1920 for its ratification. In early January 1921 the annual session of the Congress, with C.R. Das shifting over to Gandhi, not only confirmed support for Non-Cooperation, but established a new constitution with a mechanism for day-to-day work of the Congress and providing for mass membership within linguistic areas. Above all, it proclaimed 'the aim of attainment of Swarajya by all legitimate and peaceful means'. Gandhi's creed had become the creed of the Congress.

The Non-Cooperation Movement showed considerable success in boycott of foreign cloth, exodus from government educational institutions and abstention from council elections. This was accompanied by much labour unrest and peasant upsurges, the latter often of a spontaneous kind, but deriving undoubted strength from Gandhi's reputation as a protector of the poor. Given Gandhi's faith in accommodating the interests of zamindars and peasants, his 'Instructions' to U.P. peasants (February 1921) are understandable. He urged restraint (no non-payment of rent and tax; no unlawful action) since 'we are not at the present moment offering Civil Disobedience'; and he counselled a course that might 'turn zamindars into friends'. But it is heavy exaggeration to say that he thereby called for abandonment of the peasant movement. Gandhi, even in the 'Instructions', throughout identifies himself with the peasants, who appear in first-person plural ('we'), while the zamindars are treated as outsiders ('they'). Hindu–Muslim unity, and the spurning of caste hierarchy and untouchability are emphasized; these were surely essential building-blocks for any unified and conscious (not segmented and purely spontaneous) peasant movement in India.

As, despite arrests, the Non-Cooperation Movement gained momentum and the peasant began to awaken, Gandhi was promising Swaraj within a year; in October 1921 the Congress Working Committee called on Indians to desist from serving as civilians or soldiers under the British, and authorized 'Civil Disobedience', a measure confirmed by the Ahmedabad Congress in December. Gandhi was to begin it with a no-tax campaign in Bardoli district when, on 4 February 1922, the killing of policemen by peasants at Chauri Chaura persuaded him to withdraw the entire movement (12 February). Gandhi explained this decision as arising out of his discovery that Indians had not yet learnt to be non-violent. It may, however, be argued that he was fearful of a brutal government response to Chauri Chaura, with the support of zamindars and their henchmen; the Congress resolution of 12 February gave a specific assurance to the zamindars that rents would be paid and their legal rights respected. The withdrawal of the movement left it practically without any gains. The cause of Khilafat and Turkey was abandoned, though here enough had been done to inhibit Britain from risking its position in India by intervening in Turkey when Kamal Ataturk began his offensive against the Greeks in May 1922. But Swaraj still remained as distant as before.

Gandhi's decision immediately created a rift in the Congress leadership and a general demoralization began, which C.R. Das and Motilal Nehru tried to stem by returning to the politics of parliamentary opposition (Congress-Swaraj Party). The Khilafatists, by and large, began to disintegrate. Gandhi had his own band of 'No-Changers' (Rajagopalachari, Vallabhbhai Patel, etc.) who opposed council entry, but their influence too was on the decline. The British Government created one of its major tactical blunders now by arresting Gandhi (10 March 1922) and putting him on trial. Gandhi entered a defiant plea of 'guilty' to the charge of spreading 'disaffection' against His Majesty and thanked the judge for classing him with Tilak while sentencing him to six years' imprisonment. He was, however, released early in February 1924, owing to illness.

During the period of his imprisonment the Swarajists had established themselves, despite an initial reverse at the Gaya Congress (1922). With growing demoralization and the growth of communal differences, the possibility of reviving 'Civil Disobedience' seemed correspondingly to recede. Gandhi, confronting the worsening communal situation, gave frank expression to his feelings, which hurt both Arya Samajists and Muslim leaders. Discretion might have suggested a different course; but Gandhi seldom heeded the advice of prudence against the immediate urging of his conscience. Then he went on a twenty-one-day fast (despite ill health) on 18 September 1924 as a 'penance' to restore Hindu–Muslim unity. There is little doubt, however, that with the revival of Malaviya's Hindu Mahasabha and the establish-

ment of the RSS (1925), on the one hand, and the increasingly communal nature of the utterances of the Ali brothers and some other Muslim leaders, on the other, the great religious divide, which Gandhi had
always feared, seemed to rend apart the National Movement. The Swaraj
Party, by concentrating on 'council entry', perforce addressed only a
privileged section and had little to offer to the '98 per cent' of whom
C.R. Das had spoken; it failed, therefore, to stem the communal tide as
well as the erosion of its own mass support.

Could Gandhi offer something different? He began to restate his
views with increasing invocation of an egalitarian approach. He advocated an optional universal suffrage (1924). He was ready to be a
'socialist', believing in state ownership of such machine industry as
had to be permitted; he was not averse to being even a 'Bolshevik',
though his Bolshevism was different from that of M.N. Roy, the Communist leader, whom he gave space to in Young India (1925). In regard
to the caste system he moved with great care, as, for example, in his
speech at the Untouchability Conference (1924). He totally opposed
untouchability and demanded equality for untouchables; yet, though
himself eating with them, he denied he was advocating caste inter-
dining or inter-marriage. He continued to proclaim his adherence to
a varnashrama of his own interpretation. Clearly, Gandhi was trying to
target untouchability and so bring the poorest of the poor into the
National Movement without provoking the other castes, who constituted the majority. Naicker and Ambedkar would scoff at the internal
contradictions of Gandhi's logic; but it fitted into the Sarvodaya scheme
of his, where the interests of all were to be accommodated. So too was
his promotion of 'cow protection' without coercing Muslims and
Christians, or of temple entry for the low castes, as in the Vaikkom
Satyagraha (1925), without affecting the established ritual and priestly
domination. Gandhi hesitated for long in saying that men and women
are equal; but he made women the major tools of his khadi movement,
as spinners, to protect Indian hand-spun and hand-woven cloth, and
so sustain Swadeshi and the boycott of foreign cloth. Women, therefore, became an essential component of his army of workers; and one
can see him becoming more and more uncompromising over their
position as time passed.

What is important in what Gandhi was doing is not surely the limitations of his social message. The importance is that he made the achievement of social equality, admittedly at an elementary level, a cardinal part of the objectives of the National Movement, as no previous leader had done. Gandhi's 'Constructive programme' involved the movement of khadi-clad men and women to villages, promoting spinning, undertaking education and fighting untouchability. However limited, it was often for the first time that the poorest had thus been cared for, not as recipients of charity but as equals. In the North-West Frontier, Khan Abdul Ghaffar Khan independently began a similar movement ('Khudai Khidmatgars') among Pathans, and then recognized Gandhi as his teacher and leader. Gandhi was thus creating with labour and skill a mass-base for the National Movement, whose strength was perhaps first shown in the Bardoli Satyagraha of 1928, a successful struggle of peasants against tax enhancements.

A radical wind began to blow in the Congress with the boycott of the Simon Commission (1927) and disappointment with the moderate scheme of the Motilal Nehru Report (1928). Gandhi instinctively supported the strategy of moderation, but took an important step of building bridges with the radicals by unexpectedly proposing Jawaharlal Nehru's name as President of the Congress for its Lahore session, to be held December 1929. At Lahore the Congress proclaimed its aim of 'Purna Swaraj' and launched a Civil Disobedience Movement for its attainment. It was to be led by Gandhi.

Gandhi began with a moderate statement of eleven points, including reduction of land revenue, reduction of army expenditure, abolition of salt tax, rupee devaluation, protective tariffs, prohibition, etc., which were designed to appeal to different sections from peasants to businessmen, and still taking care not to hurt the landlords. Gandhi singled out the salt monopoly as the initial target of Civil Disobedience, signalled by his month-long Dandi March, reaching Dandi on 5 April 1930 to launch the Salt Saryagraha. As arrests of Congress leaders and workers began, a mass upsurge developed in many parts of the country. Government authority collapsed in Peshawar for nearly ten days (24 April to 5 May). On 5 May Gandhi was himself arrested. A mass Civil Disobedience followed. The government responded by imprisoning over 90,000 resisters (including large numbers of women), and seizing and selling away peasants' properties for withholding payments of tax. The Civil Disobedience was 'discontinued' with the Gandhi–Irwin Agreement of 4 March 1931. The euphoria over the Viceroy signing a treaty with the leader of the Indian nation had, however, to be tempered by the fact that, apart from the release of prisoners and the lifting of the ban on Congress organizations, no substantial gain had resulted. Much of the sequestered property would not be released; and the great national hero, Bhagat Singh, could not be saved from the gallows.

It is almost certain that Gandhi wanted to have a settlement before the Civil Disobedience lost its momentum. Perhaps, the embarrassment of an unfavourable truce partly explains Gandhi's major ideological concessions at the Karachi Congress convened on 29 March 1931. The Fundamental Rights Resolution approved at Karachi was drafted by Jawaharlal Nehru, but revised by Gandhi. It contained some reflection of Gandhi's major concerns, but essentially it envisioned a modern democratic welfare-state, not a state based on self-help; an industrial society, not a pre-industrial, rural one; enforcement of equality between men and women and prohibition of untouchability by law, not by persuasion; protection of labour and reduction of rent and reform of tenure (so, possibly, an abolition of zamindari, not explicitly called for), with no place for the conception of industrialists and landlords as 'custodians' of the poor. The Resolution was a total reversal of Gandhi's 1909 vision of 'Hind Swaraj'. Perhaps, Gandhi realized that he himself had helped to unleash forces within Indian society that were demanding their due place, not according to a modified version of the traditional order, but in consonance with more uncompromising notions derived from bourgeois democracy, if not socialism.

Gandhi's participation in the Second Round Table Conference in London in 1931, as a result of the Gandhi–Irwin Agreement, was a matter of great personal stress for him. While he and the Congress were willing to accept separate electorates for the Muslims and Sikhs, the leaders of the motley groups of communal organizations invited to the Conference looked more towards sectional concessions from British imperialism than accommodation with the Congress; and the Conference broke up without anything being achieved. As the inevitable resumption of Civil Disobedience followed this impasse, the government responded by arresting Gandhi on 4 January 1932, banning the Congress organizations, seizing their funds and assets, with 32,458 convicted prisoners officially reported in April. Having so disposed of their main opponent, the British Government announced a Communal Award (4 August) in which the depressed castes were given a separate electorate. Gandhi responded with a fast (20 September) against both untouchability and the separation of depressed castes. This led to the Poona Pact between depressed-caste and caste-Hindu leaders (24 September), which forced the British Cabinet to amend the Communal Award accordingly, and Gandhi was thereby able to break his fast in prison on 26 September. Characteristically, he now began to emphasize the promises caste Hindus had made about equal rights to the untouchables (now christened 'Harijans' by Gandhi). He combined Civil Disobedience (and so recurrent imprisonments) with a strong campaign against untouchability, leading to another long fast in May 1933. Many Congress leaders regarded this campaign as a diversion from the main business of Civil Disobedience; but it is also probable that it was this concentration on the major division in Indian society that enabled the National Movement to keep and expand its social base. The Civil Disobedience, however, could hardly be maintained; already suspended by Gandhi in May 1933, it was finally withdrawn in April 1934. Gandhi himself 'retired' from the Congress; but this was a formal dissociation, and he remained the final arbiter in all the major decisions of the Congress.

Gandhi made Wardha his headquarters, shifting from Ahmedabad, and occupied himself energetically with the rural programme whose essential elements he had worked out in the 1920s. By 1934 the All-India Spinners' Association served 5,300 villages, giving employment to 2,20,000 female spinners, 20,000 weavers and 20,000 carders. The *Harijan*, replacing *Young India*, became the organ of the Village-Industries Association, representing the combination of rural uplift with the fight against untouchability. It cannot be doubted that these Gandhian 'NGOs' relied for crucial financial support on men of big business, like G.D. Birla, but the spartan austerity Gandhi promoted made their workers so identify themselves with the rural poor that they continued to broaden mass support for the Congress even where they had only been heard about, not seen.

But a parallel movement was also growing apace. In 1934 Gandhi recognized that the socialist ideas, 'however distasteful some of them may be to me', had a right to be represented; but he warned against their 'gain[ing] ascendancy' in the Congress. The All-India Kisan Sabha, with a strongly left orientation, had its first conference in April 1936, and in 1935 the All-India Trade Union Congress virtually passed under Communist leadership. This, for the first time, presented a challenge to Gandhi, who was not willing to let the National Movement become involved in internal class struggles, whereas to the Left it appeared that mass support could be gained precisely by organizing peasants and workers for their rights. The rift was, however, glossed over constantly by Gandhi's personal support to Nehru, who in these years was the principal spokesman for the vision of a socialist India.

The Congress success in 1937, with the enlarged electorate created by the Act of 1935, was certainly owing to the joining of both the streams, the Gandhian and the Left, votes being sought for the Congress on a manifesto which reproduced the Karachi Resolution of 1931. Gandhi supported the taking of office and the forming of provincial ministries, but he left much of the control and guidance of the Congress ministries to Nehru and Subhas Bose (Congress President, 1938), though both had opposed the acceptance of office. The All-India Congress Committee in 1937 also accepted 'Hindi-Hindustani' as the language of the Congress, on Gandhi's insistence that Hindustani was the correct name of 'Urdu'. This involved him in an unfortunate controversy with Urdu supporters, giving grist to the communal mill. Later on, Gandhi himself began giving pride of place to Hindustani as the language that embraced both Hindi and Urdu. Had this position been taken by him originally, much disputation could have been avoided and the Muslim League not allowed another point to justify its tirades against the Congress. Around this time Gandhi developed a scheme for basic education, given detailed shape in the Report of the Zakir Husain Committee (1937), setting the aim of free compulsory school education in the mother-tongue, to be combined with vocational training. This became known as the Wardha Scheme, and it was intended that the Congress provincial governments would also give active support to it. In the working of the Congress ministries Gandhi was firm in insisting on civil liberties and on the release of political prisoners, despite the risk of losing office on the Governor's refusal in

U.P. (February 1938). The Governor's capitulation on the issue was a notable nationalist gain. Unfortunately, however, Gandhi does not seem to have pressed similarly for ameliorative measures like tenancy reform and labour legislation; and this led to a crisis at the Tripuri Congress session where a majority of delegates, disenchanted with his stance, re-elected Subhas Bose as President against Gandhi's candidate, Sitaramayya (29 January 1939). Yet Gandhi's leadership was specifically recognized by the same session, and Bose was soon compelled to resign.

As World War II broke out on 3 September 1939, the Congress refused to associate itself in the war effort and the ministries resigned. This was not because Gandhi had any neutral feelings about Hitler and Nazism. He had never sympathized with Hitler and had condemned the persecution of the Jews by the Nazis, while supporting the Palestinian Arabs against Zionism. Nor did he agree with the Communist perception of the war in its first phase (1939–41) as being inter-imperialist in nature. But he felt that the British Government should make important commitments in return for cooperation; and this not coming about, as shown by the Viceroy's 'August offer' of 1940, he initiated an individual Saryagraha, beginning in October 1940. By June 1941, when Hitler invaded the Soviet Union, about 20,000 had gone to jail.

The German attack on the Soviet Union and the Japanese entry into the war by the end of the year (1941) dramatically changed the complexion of the war. Yet the British Government, through the Cripps Mission (March–April 1942), made no substantive immediate concessions and furnished only vague promises for the future. In the meantime, the Allied position both in Asia and Europe became increasingly difficult. The Germans were on the verge of reaching the Volga for the crucial battle of Stalingrad; the Japanese had come up to the Indian frontier. It seemed to Gandhi that it was essential to support the Allied effort; but, given the situation of the Allies, a massive non-violent Satyagraha could succeed in forcing Britain to make important political concessions. The 'Quit India' Resolution on 8 August 1942 was the result of this understanding of the world situation. (Nehru is reported to have admitted: 'It is Gandhiji's feeling that Japan and Germany will win'.) Churchill gave Gandhi and the Congress no time to frame tactics to accord with circumstances. A stream of repression was let loose: spontaneous acts of peaceful and violent protest alike were suppressed by armed power, and nearly 92,000 people, including Gandhi (arrested on 9 August), were put in prison. While one acclaims the courage of the rebels of 1942, and cannot doubt the sincerity of Gandhiji and the national leaders, it is difficult to escape the conclusion that the Quit India Resolution was based on a huge miscalculation about the world situation. The Red Army, by defeating Hitler at Stalingrad (January 1943) and reversing the tide of war, to that extent freed British imperialism from the necessity of making any immediate concessions in India. It is another matter that the very victory over Nazism and Japan by an alliance in which the Soviet Union had played a crucial role, ultimately also meant that Britain could no longer rule its empire in the old way.

Gandhi lost his wife during his imprisonment and went on fast against the Viceroy's accusation that he had contemplated violence (February 1943). Serious illness led to his release in May 1944. While Gandhi had been in prison, the Muslim League had gained in strength. Its Lahore Resolution (1940) had demanded a separate Muslim state or states, and it was now propagating the slogan of 'Pakistan'. Gandhi made a serious effort to negotiate a compromise of the kind that he had made many times previously to placate communal aspirations. But the Gandhi–Jinnah talks (September 1944) failed to deliver results; and this became a precedent for practically all the tortuous negotiations that now followed, until the moment of the Mountbatten Declaration dividing India in 1947. All the Congress leaders were released early in 1945. It was clear from the responses to the INA trials and the RIN Mutiny (February 1946), and the Congress sweep in the 1946 elections, that Indian freedom could not be delayed. India's unity, however, also came into question. In order to preserve the country's unity, Gandhi was often prepared to give concessions to the Muslim League beyond what his colleagues would concede. For this he received only spiteful words of contempt from both the Muslim Leaguers and the Hindu Mahasabhaites.

In the last phase of his life Gandhi did his best to save the people from the communal carnage that began with the Muslim League's Direct Action Day at Calcutta, 16 August 1946. Gandhi pursued the communal fire, trying to quench it in Noakhali (East Bengal), Bihar and Calcutta, bravely facing both Muslim and Hindu mobs. He quietly let 15 August 1947 pass and subsequently went on fast, near a Muslim slum at Calcutta, to stop the post-Partition slaughter in the great city. The people of Calcutta at last responded, and he moved to Delhi (14 September) to confront the far larger scale of carnage in the then Punjab and Delhi. He faced hostile audiences, which even forced the abandonment of his prayer since the Quran would not be allowed to be recited. All his appeals and persuasion seemed to be unavailing, till at last he began his fast (13 January 1948) for peace and, additionally, for a payment of Rs 55 crore due to Pakistan, which the Government of India had refused to pay. What Gandhi had decided to do went flagrantly against the current stream. At first his fast met with hostile local reception; but then the popular conscience was aroused, and the rioters and their mentors were increasingly isolated. Gandhi laid down detailed conditions for the safety of Muslims in Delhi before he would abandon his fast. When full assurances were received and the Government of India announced the payment of dues to Pakistan, Gandhi broke his fast (18 January).

Gandhi's success in stopping riots in Delhi, and asserting the need for friendly relations between India and Pakistan – he insisted he belonged to both – generated a genuine popular aversion to mutual slaughter in both countries. If one has to choose any single act as the most singularly consequential by that great man, this was surely it. It was also to prove his death-warrant. Preparing to go to Pakistan to further his mission of amity, Gandhi was shot down on the way to his Prayer Meeting, at Delhi, on 30 January 1948. The assassin was Nathuram Godse, a man with RSS and Hindu Mahasabha antecedents and connections. And he was not alone in the plot.

2

Gandhi and the National Movement

Anyone who is seriously interested in Indian history must be confronted in his own mind with the nature of the National Movement, which could be regarded as the greatest creation of the Indian people to date, and, inescapably along with it, the nature of Gandhi's legacy. I should like to begin with my own first encounter with the problem of assessment of Gandhiji. Though it may appear to be of a rather personal character, my difficulties were not probably exceptional. They might have been faced by many who came to the Communist movement during the last phase of the National Movement. With my parents it was usual to refer to Gandhi not as Gandhiji, but only as Mahatmaji; even to refer to him as Gandhiji was thought of as taking a liberty. It did not mean that my father was not critical of certain positions taken by Gandhiji: but it meant that, whatever the criticism, it was within a framework in which Gandhiji's total dominance of the National Movement was taken for granted, so that although one might differ from him, one must defer to his views. From this background, suddenly to encounter references in Communist literature – notably R.P. Dutt's *India Today* – to his being the 'mascot of the bourgeoisie', 'that general of unbroken disasters', 'the Jonah of Revolution', came as a personal shock. One tended to attribute this sense of shock to one's own petty-bourgeois psychology, but this excuse did not stamp out

This lecture, dedicated to the memory of Safdar Hashmi, was given in 1995. A revised transcript of its text was published in *Social Scientist*, Vol. 23, Nos. 4–6, 1995.

one's discomfort; and the dissatisfaction with such an assessment of Gandhiji persisted.

It later seemed to me, while re-reading R.P. Dutt, that even within his attack on Gandhi there were important concessions – the admission, for example, that Gandhi alone could enter the huts and hearts of the Indian poor, where the Indian bourgeoisie could never gain entrance. How and why did he obtain this particular ability? Any explanation of how Gandhi achieved this rapport with the Indian poor and with the Indian people as a whole was missing in R.P. Dutt's analysis. I think that subsequent Left assessments of Gandhiji became difficult because of a particular misconception of its own position in the National Movement by the Left. The Left not only decried the bourgeois leadership of the National Movement and its various limitations, but tried to suggest as if the Left movement ran parallel to, and not as part of, the National Movement. R.P. Dutt, indeed, thought of the working-class movement and the Communist movement as essentially sections of the National Movement, in which they were contesting with the bourgeoisie for leadership. But in certain writings of E.M.S. Namboodiripad, for example, notably his latest collection of articles on the freedom struggle which are built upon a reading of Tara Chand's *History of the Freedom Movement* and certain other writings, it seems in fact as if there were three parties to the struggle, viz. imperialism, bourgeois nationalism and the working-class movement. The Subaltern historians take this to another extreme in which the whole National Movement is seen as an elitist movement. The 'subaltern' classes, according to this theory, consisting of the zamindars and other rural, unmodernized strata, possessed a unique autonomy, and based on this autonomy they contested for power with imperialism; whereas the national elite merely benefited from their struggle and, instead of transferring power to the subalterns, they transferred power to themselves. Therefore, in a sense, imperialism and nationalism were of the same category, or belonged to the same class more or less, viz. the westernized elite, while the subalterns who carried out the autonomous struggles would, as was almost fatally inevitable, lose out. It was on the basis of their autonomous struggles that the leadership of the National Movement took power from Britain. This puts the Communist movement, along with the nationalist leadership, in the same nasty elitist basket. Then, because you have the term subaltern on one side, you do not have the bourgeoisie on the other side, you only have elites – and whether they are imperialist elites or nationalist elites, it does not apparently much matter.

The Subalterns are so satisfied with their theology that Gandhi is not very relevant to them, and although we are told by some scholars that Subaltern studies have opened a new vision on Gandhi, I have not been blessed with receiving that kind of insight from them. It seems to me that lumping everyone in one basket of undifferentiated elites, or very thinly differentiated elites, and treating the subalterns as autonomous, which means denying the influence of Gandhi on those vast classes of the Indian poor, is a position no person aware of the reality in any measure can accept. Indeed, if one starts with this denial, then, of course, one cannot offer any real perception of Gandhi.

Imperialist historians, including British Government officials during the British period, and post-Independence British historians thereafter, have always tried to argue that Gandhi was only a Mahatma to look at from outside; otherwise he was a very clever politician, a master of manipulation, and that the British in a sense themselves created the myth of Gandhi with their own actions, both constitutional and political. Those who are familiar with Anil Seal's work would remember that, according to him, the nationalist appeal did not acquire any popular support till the elections of 1937, because it was the Government of India Act 1935, rather than Gandhi's and other nationalist mobilizations, which gave Indian politicians the necessary impetus to reach out to the Indian masses. As for those who, in the Civil Disobedience Movement of 1930–31, risked their lives and property for Indian freedom at Gandhi's call, Judith Brown has already put them in their place: they were merely Gandhi's 'sub-contractors' or 'intermediaries'. Their's was thus a business enterprise, no real movement. So, not Gandhism, nor any other strand in the National Movement, Left or any other, but the constitutional measures of the British Government, particularly the Government of India Act 1935, created that massive nationalist following among the Indian people. The application of the Namierist method by the Cambridge School, Seal, Brown and others, results, as has been said about its application to English history, in a simple loss of the wood for the trees. I particularly remember the facts that Seal tells us about Dadabhai Naoroji's personal financial problems, but one will never realize from Seal that Naoroji wrote papers over time which, collected together, became almost the nationalist bible on the economic role of imperialism. He has no explanation why Naoroji continued to be supported by Bombay mill-owners even when he declined to support them in their opposition to the passage of industrial labour legislation. That ideas have a momentum of their own is a fact which the Cambridge school and its supporters so easily overlook. There are thus such obvious imperfections in their approach to Gandhi that I need not dilate on them any further.

 We are then favoured also by a psychoanalysis of Gandhi, as for example undertaken by Erikson and Kakar, where particularly his relations with his mother are emphasized, and for some reason Indian culture is itself described as feminine. I have not been able to see how this gender characterization of any culture is possible. Such an approach, which is Eurocentric and psychological, results in an obvious depreciation and belittling of Gandhi's importance.

The nationalist literature about Gandhiji is considerable; much of it is also academically important, and contains criticism here and there. Tara Chand's *History of the Freedom Movement* has certain criticisms, for example, on Gandhi's role in the Second Round Table Conference. So one cannot dismiss this entire body of literature as mere adulation. But by emphasizing Gandhi's immense achievement as a person, and not relating it to the social environment and the historical situation, this body of literature, though important (and one must remember that most of the massive literature on Gandhi comes from this large body of work), is not very satisfying to me in its total perception. Partly, this is because its conception of social development is not one which I share. But essentially I think one has an inward reservation about it because the focus is so much on Gandhi, that the people of India for whom he worked and died appear merely as obedient admirers. Now, with this rather arrogant criticism, for which I apologize, of various historical interpretations, I would like to go on to my provisional views; and, as I describe these, I think the major questions that I pose would also emerge.

First of all, I would argue that Gandhiji's autobiography, *My Experiments with Truth*, is exceptionally important for us. It is so honest that perhaps, of all great figures in modern history, Gandhi should most easily become the victim of Freudian psychoanalysis. But while I would accept every fact that Gandhiji gives of himself, and as he gives it – and of the most dramatic events he is perhaps the dullest narrator – yet I would argue that he is perhaps not the best authority or source for our own perception of the genesis of his thought. For example, he always described himself as a Sanatani Hindu, yet he did not pray in a temple.

The basic point is that the serious body of thought that Gandhi first came into contact with was modern, western thought. It was not traditional Hindu philosophy. It was after his modern education at Rajkot and at London that he even read the *Bhagvad Gita* (and that too in England and in an English translation). While he may have joined a vegetarian society and might have come into contact with Theosophists – although one understands that his major contact with Theosophists, that also of not a long duration, was in South Africa, in Durban – it was essentially Victorian England's liberal values that Gandhi assimilated when he was in England. These influences were strong enough for him to go to France when the centenary celebrations of the French Revolution took place in 1889.

We know that when he went to South Africa in the early 1890s, to stay there with some small breaks for twenty-one years, he began reading Ruskin and Tolstoy and other western thinkers. His criticism of certain features of both western and Indian civilizations came mainly from a reading of modern European writing. I do not think there is in the mass of Indian tradition such an emphasis on dignity of labour as he was later to attribute to it, but which he himself admittedly derived from a reading of Ruskin, whose book *Unto This Last* he translated into Gujarati under the title *Sarvodaya*. His emphasis on peace, and not war, as the only legitimate means of settling political issues came from Tolstoy rather than any Indian tradition. In the Indian tradition *ahimsa* is seen more as abstaining from the taking of life and, therefore, a logical step to vegetarianism. It has not been, in traditional Indian thought, perceived as a means of carrying out a revolution. Therefore the essential strands in Gandhi's own intellectual make-up are certainly modern, which is a very important point to remember. Gandhi recognized the debt he owed to the western thinkers, whose works he read. He was too honest a man not to extend them this recognition.

But his own belief that these writings merely strengthened, merely underlined, merely reinforced what was present in his mind, perhaps dormant, as an inheritance from India's own tradition, must necessarily be doubted.

Now clearly having found this body of thought which appealed to him, which rejected capitalism as the creation of the modern western civilization, which rejected imperialism that had established itself through war and massacres, Gandhi was led to reject western civilization itself nearly wholesale. This rejection became the starting-point for asserting the superiority of Indian civilization, which neither possessed capitalism nor had taken to imperialism. So the very poverty of Indian civilization in material terms became, for Gandhi, the ground for asserting its superiority.

This process was a very complex one, and the complexities and the contradictions are apparent in Gandhi's major work, *Hind Swaraj*, written on a voyage from England to South Africa in 1909. Already by the time of *Hind Swaraj*, Gandhi's internal perception of the genesis of his own thought is apparently complete. He reads into the *Bhagvad Gita* that, which it may seem to one, is not there. He reads a message of duty, a message of dignity of labour; he reads a message of peace. He was similarly to assert, equally unhistorically, that the message of peace can be read as strongly in the Quran. Gandhi's words often seem much more a restatement of the New Testament than of either the *Bhagvad Gita* or the Quran. They are not to be seen as an assertion of the traditional against modern values. What we get is the assertion of modern values in traditional garb, a re-reading of Indian culture in a totally ahistorical, but extremely creative fashion. Something of it was there in the Bengal Renaissance, in Ram Mohun Roy's appeal to the Upanishads and in his appeal to certain legal books which gave some inheritance rights to women. In Gandhi's case the statement of modern values in traditional terms was far more complete and far more extensive, although, for this reason, the contradictions within such unnatural convergence were also very glaring.

Gandhi's reading of Indian culture cannot be justified by any historical reading of the texts. But what he was ascribing to Hinduism or Islam – his ascriptions to Islam were, of course, comparatively fewer – were the principles he himself had in mind with regard to Hinduism, an ascription which has so greatly contributed to the remoulding of Hinduism in its present form. One of the achievements of Gandhi is, I think, that he changed the course of Hinduism or at least gave a new face to Hinduism, even when all the time he was saying that he was merely asserting its ancient values. Ultimately, and over a long process, he would accept a position of traditional Hinduism, only to undermine it: for example, his acceptance first of the *varna* principle in the *Hind Swaraj* and then his steady undermining of it until almost nothing remained of it by the 1940s. Or, his acceptance first of a special position for women only in the house, as implied in the *Hind Swaraj*, and then his undermining of it till, in the 1940s, he was arguing – I still remember an interview of a newspaper correspondent with Gandhi in 1945–46 – for the equality of women in practically all aspects of life. Gandhi clearly said that he not only believed in the equality of men and women, but that women could do all the things that men could do and men would not be able to do all the things that women do. The correspondent asked Gandhi that if *ahimsa* permitted war, could women be soldiers; and Gandhi said they would be better soldiers and generals than men. Maybe there are certain other statements of his which militate against this, but generally the tone of Gandhi's later thought is to reject any kind of inequality between man and woman.

Then there is his emphasis on monotheism when he was all the time denying this emphasis. He would say that he was a Sanatani Hindu and on this basis he would support the movement of the Untouchables to enter temples, and yet, unlike today's politicians, in his personal life he never gave concession to anything short of monotheism. In effect he tended to make Hinduism more of a monothestic religion than did even the Arya Samajists, with whom, of course, he did not agree. He also ascribed to Hinduism a degree of tolerance which perhaps in its history it had not possessed, and, therefore, tried to make it a more tolerant religion. In this sense he was working on the same lines as his precursors like Ram Mohun Roy, Keshavchandra Sen and Justice Ranade. Perhaps he was the last of these men, and also the greatest of them undoubtedly. By attributing all his statements to roots in the Indian civilization, and particularly in Hinduism, he created a picture of Hinduism which made it possible for its followers to accept modern values. As seen by Gandhi, it is a religion that has nothing in common with the current 'Hindutva' cult. Gandhi's Ram was God, and his Ram Rajya did not relate to something that was remotely sectarian. 'God's Rule' would be a better translation of it. It bore the same sense in which Kabir referred to Ram. Clearly, then, even Gandhi's religiosity was based on an extension of humanitarian values and their application to what is perhaps the most ancient of all surviving religions, resulting in a vast transformation of its beliefs. Many of those who once thought that the caste system was basic to Hinduism, would, by the year of Gandhi's death, have been annoyed if anyone were to refer to it as an essential part of Hinduism. This was the extent of Gandhi's achievement in relation to the theological tenets of Hinduism.

My main point here is to assert that Gandhi is a modern thinker. Those who would like to designate thought in class terms are welcome to call him a bourgeois thinker. But I would like to remind such critics of a peculiar idiosyncrasy of Karl Marx. When he encounters an economist who has not thought properly, who is a vulgarizer, or has capitalists' current interests directly in mind, he always calls him a bourgeois economist. But as far as the two principal great economists, Adam Smith and Ricardo, are concerned, it is always of their classical political economy that he speaks. I would, therefore, rather think of Gandhi as a 'classical' modern figure. If still bourgeois, then not in the sense of a personal classification, but defined by the end to which his social and political strategy, despite his own subjective intentions, was bound finally to take the historical movement he led. 'Bourgeois', in any case, even as a designation, represents no single body of thought; and I think we are beginning to recognize that socialist, proletarian thought cannot be a single body of consistent thought either. There could be, and were, different strands of classical bourgeois thought – and his was one strand. Although Gandhi's thought-content was anti-imperialist and subjectively anti-capitalist (because anti-industrial), nevertheless, since he did not extend his aims to socialism, he essentially remained within the bourgeois framework of thought.

With regard to the National Movement I think, again, some points need to be stressed. The National Movement in India had already begun, already established itself, when Gandhi entered the political field in South Africa. The founding fathers of the National Movement had a level of critique of imperialism which one can only admire today. Dadabhai Naoroji and R.C. Dutt wrote on the economic role of imperialism in India, which later Marxist writing largely followed, without any major improvement, during the British rule. They underscored the modern imperialist exploitation of India. But they implicitly underscored one other important point – that the National Movement can only create a modern India. There cannot be any going back to Ancient India, and, therefore, India did not only need education, it needed a new ideology. This ideology they sought to create through various kinds of movements like the Brahmo Samaj; and I would like to recall here that in 1828 Ram Mohun Roy said that India cannot generate 'patriotism' because the people are divided up among many castes. If India had to be a nation, then the caste system had to be rejected. I think Keshavchandra Sen must be particularly respected because he extended this view of social liberation also to the repression of women, and in 1870 propounded the idea that as India reformed itself it would become a nation. So India was not historically a nation. It was making itself into a nation by rejecting its inherited past, that of a society divided according to castes and religions. It could make itself into a nation also by rejecting the traditional oppression of women, by absorbing modern thought and trying to develop a modern capitalist economy. The *swadeshi*, or the development of the internal Indian economy, in their minds was directed towards an industrial capitalist economy, the only kind of advanced economy they saw functioning around them. Dadabhai Naoroji may have been drawn towards the socialists because the socialists were anti-imperialists, and he might also have been drawn to labour legislation, but essentially his notion of the future of India, and also that of R.C. Dutt, was what can be called capitalism 'with a human face', in Mr Narasimha Rao's phraseology, but with more substance.

The second important thing about Gandhi was his desire to unite the National Movement with economic struggles. The earlier thinkers among the Moderates had provided the intellectual material for it. They had shown how India was being exploited by England, but in their actual politics they acted merely as self-appointed spokesmen of the Indian people. They made demands on behalf of the Indian poor, but they were unable to spread these very ideas among the masses whose cause they espoused. They spoke of banning exports of Indian foodgrains, but there were no demonstrations of hungry, famine-stricken people supporting this demand. There was practically no popular mobilization. With Gandhi one enters an important phase in the National Movement, when mobilization for rectification of economic grievances became a part of the National Movement. It seems to me that this is an extremely important achievement, which is by no means diminished by the fact that the earlier demands behind such mobilizations tended to be extremely moderate.

But then, nowhere in the world does a serious trade union start with the most radical demands. It always starts with the demand, say, that temporary employees be made regular employees; it is only later, as workers gain in confidence, that they begin to make ambitious demands about pay and promotion, and a voice in management. Certainly any trade union which, according to the wishes of the Subalterns and other such radicals, have a strike every day, would have a very short life in the working-class movement. Clearly, the necessarily limited nature of day-to-day demands and the ability to compromise are an inalienable part of any serious peasant and working-class movement. When we say that Gandhi in the Champaran Satyagraha in 1917 was merely leading rich peasants, this is an important point to consider. Certainly it should be found out who were mainly affected; but, first of all, we ought to recall that Gandhi did not lead them because he thought they were rich peasants. Second, it was clear that the demands had to be narrow because without any partial success the Satyagraha would have had a totally demoralizing effect. So also in the Kheda Satyagraha and the Ahmedabad working-class strike: the complaints that the demands were limited, that compromises were entered into, are not serious criticisms. Even the greatest Marxists would have done the same. They may perhaps have not gone on hunger strike, but at some stage they would have had to compromise. One could not, in one agitation, have overthrown the landlord system in India, or the capitalist system in Ahmedabad, or the British rule in Champaran or in Kheda district.

Another important achievement, as I see, in Gandhi is his immediate identification with the peasantry. He might use religious language for it, which one may deplore, but the essential point remains that to him the peasants were those with whom he identified himself most. I have been amused to read in *Subaltern Studies*, Volume I, an analysis of a document in which Gandhi is supposed to have abandoned the peasants and made a compromise with the zamindars. Although the 'subaltern' author does not quote R.P. Dutt, the approach here is identical: Gandhi had made a compromise with zamindars, he had surrendered to zamindars in 1922, forced the peasant to retreat and so on. But in interpreting this 'discourse' – and these are interpreters who look at each word – the Subalterns forget that when Gandhi used the word 'we' in this document he meant peasants and when he used 'they' he meant the zamindars, thus indicating essentially an element of differentiation from the zamindars and solidarity with the peasant masses of the country.

Now one can argue that this was false identification, that he was not in fact representing the peasants' long-term interests. (Let us forget about the temporary compromise because as far as compromises are concerned, I have argued that they are essential in any movement.) In the long term Gandhi was talking about zamindars as trustees, as custodians of peasants, who should be paid rent so that they open schools and hospitals. This was, of course, impractical idealism in the extreme. But he was still raising a fresh issue. First of all, rent could be reduced, a matter about which Ram Mohun Roy had also written, but very cautiously. For Gandhi rents could be reduced by peaceful methods, by negotiation, but rent taken was to be justified only if it was spent on health and education. Why should a zamindar collect rent if he was not able to enjoy it? This meant that even the idea of trusteeship brought into question the rights of the zamindars in an indirect manner. And one should also remember that in the 1920s, while peasants might rise here and there, the general situation was not of unrestrained revolt. One cannot read into the peasant movement of 1919–22 the state of the peasant's mind ten years later, which was partly also the result of the work of the Left in the 1930s. It would be absurd and it would be belittling the contribution of the Left and of Gandhi's own 'constructive' programme in the 1920s and 1930s, to consider peasant consciousness in the early 1920s at level with peasant consciousness in the 1930s. Given that position, obviously, a totally hostile attitude to the zamindars would have made the situation for the National Movement quite difficult in the early 1920s. But peasants did come into the Civil Disobedience Movement in 1930. They came to the Civil Disobedience Movement in far larger numbers than during Non-Cooperation, where their participation was relatively scattered and fragmentary. Perhaps class analysis would show that most of them were rich peasants and small zamindars. But one of the important facts does not come out well even in Sumit Sarkar's valuable work, *Modern India*. This is that when we are talking of imprisonment in the Civil Disobedience of 1930 and sneering about the fact that the number of prisoners did not exceed 1,00,000, even by Congress estimates, we are again reading into 1930 what was the position in the 1980s. Imprisonment in 1930 was not like 'political' imprisonment today, when going to prison hardly matters and it is a kind of good certificate for a political career. In fact I know of political parties who say a local leader is judged by the number of people he can bring in trucks to court arrest for one day. I remember an agitation of the CPI(M) when we had brought peasants promising them that they would be kept in prison for only one week, and unfortunately the government kept them in prison for a month. They were not angry with the government; they were angry with us. But in 1930 prison meant one could never get employment and could well lose one's property in the bargain; and therefore, one is surprised that even over 90,000 went to prison in Civil Disobedience under such circumstances. Consider losing one's land, being thrown out of one's family; and if one does that, the peasant participation in the Civil Disobedience movement all over India, and even in the North-West Frontier Province, was certainly an important event.

The suspension of Civil Disobedience in March 1931 was soon followed by the Karachi Resolution, which provided a blueprint for the industrial development of India – an objective totally opposed to Gandhi's views – under the public sector; government ownership of key industries; working-class rights and, in rather cautious terms, land to the tiller with some compensation to the zamindars; universal adult suffrage already promised in the Motilal Nehru Committee Report; equal rights to women; and separation of religion from state. Practically every modern political idea of a bourgeois welfare-state is to be found in the Karachi Resolution. The basic idea of such a state happens to coincide fairly extensively with the concept that the Communist Movement developed, post-World War II, of people's democracy as a first stage after revolution. Therefore, clearly, the Karachi Resolution is an important platform for the Left also. It united Gandhi with radicals like Nehru and with the Left. And Gandhi's acceptance (not entirely whole-hearted, it is true) of it, and his later position that he would not have any quarrel with the Congress governments which implemented it, must certainly be recognized. This was an important concession, the work of a person who could lay aside his own views and accept contrary views, because the peasants had served the Civil Disobedience Movement and deserved their reward. The working class had largely kept away from Civil Disobedience in many areas and so workers had to be attracted back to the National Movement. Women had come out to participate and they too had to have their share in the future of India. The Karachi Resolution was a kind of recognition of the requirements of a situation that Gandhi himself had helped to bring about. And so far as Gandhi allowed this to stand as part of the Congress programme, he must be credited with a very important share in helping to give to the Congress a leftward direction.

Gandhi's subsequent life, in which it became clear that free India would not be as he saw it, moved inexorably towards tragedy. He had unleashed forces, the direction of whose movement was so different from what he wanted it to be. I think in this tragedy one also recognizes his greatness, because Gandhi accepted, as I have said, in the Karachi Resolution and later, the promises that the Congress had made to the Kisans and to the Trade Unions. Gandhi recognized the direction, even while he criticized it.

In one particular respect, in the communal divide which tended to intensify again from the late 1930s, Gandhi was constantly on the side of moderation. He had not taken the view which the Left adopted in the 1930s, that if the National Movement was to be secular, then Hindu or Muslim communalism could have no place within it. It was an important position, a bold position. But it was not Gandhi's position. Tilak, before Gandhi, had brought the Congress and the Muslim League together on that classic compromise, a communal electorate for Muslims in exchange for Muslim League's acceptance of Home Rule. My friend Professor Bipan Chandra decries it as an unprincipled compromise. Yet I think it was one of the notable landmarks in the development of the National Movement. Indeed, it is fitting to recall that in 1909, in *Hind Swaraj*, Gandhi had criticized Hindu leaders for opposing the creation of communal electorates for Muslims. Gandhi himself joined the Khilafat Committee, which Abbas Tyabji, one of Gandhi's very close followers (the 'Brrr!' of his correspondence), refused to do. But Gandhi felt the Khilafat Movement would greatly extend the support base of the National Movement. On this there could always be discussion. Gandhi felt that he could ally with Muslim communalism, or indeed with Hindu communalism also, on particular issues to enlarge the National Movement. Given this argument, the Khilafat Movement was a logical development of Gandhian strategy. The criticism of separate electorates and so on came more vocally from the Left than from Gandhi, who was more willing to give concessions (from 1909 onwards, as we have seen). Indeed, in 1931, Jinnah's demands had been conceded on all the major points, but unfortunately Jinnah and the Muslim League now looked to British imperialism (and not to the National Movement) to give them these privileges. This is a very important point which some historians miss while they tend to blame the Congress and the League equally for the course that led ultimately to the Partition. It seems to me, again, that in the U.P. Cabinet issue of 1937, it was Nehru and the Left who took a more rigid position than Gandhi and Abul Kalam Azad, who were willing to induct the Muslim League ministers, even if, perhaps, in order to modify the anti-zamindar edge of Nehru's supporters. Certainly the people who mismanaged the U.P. Cabinet formation were not Gandhi's supporters, who were indeed urging a compromise. Subsequently, in 1944, C. Rajagopalachari entered into negotiations with Jinnah, and the Desai–Liaqat formula of 1945 even conceded parity: that is, the very unfair position that the Muslim League, which commanded a much smaller number of supporters by any reckoning, should have a parity in the central Cabinet with the Congress. Gandhi went to extremes in giving such concessions, in order to preserve the unity of the country.

Yet the question remains whether Gandhi, in identifying himself with Hindu social reform and with Hindus generally, antagonized Muslims. This is a question that is very difficult to answer, because, clearly, if the National Movement was to be allied with reform of social evils, which were so deeply wedded to religion, it itself could not be separated entirely from religion. One had either to speak within the religious framework for social reform, as Gandhi did, or to reject religion altogether, which is what the Left did (including Nehru as may be seen from his *Autobiography*), so as to remove the very root of old customs.

One would not know which device would have been more successful given the Indian situation. But certainly Gandhi adopted the first one; he sincerely adopted it, since he was himself deeply religious. Gandhi naturally found it very difficult to speak of social reform to Muslims, to condemn bigamy, to demand an equal share in inheritance for daughters among Muslims and so on, because Muslims believed that all these inequities were part of their religion. If he had insisted upon such reform among them, the alienation of the Muslims from him would have been still greater. And therefore, it is not also easy to condemn him on this score. He did all that could be expected of him to do, to assert that all religions were in part true, but that all religions had some errors as well. They should, therefore, exist together. Moving away from his controversial terminology of the late 1930s, he argued by 1947 that Hindustani should be the national language of India in both Devnagri and Urdu scripts. He was a promoter of the equality of Hindi and Urdu as separate forms of that language. I don't know how many know that he wrote Urdu also, and that his spelling was fairly correct. (His letters to my aunt, Raihana Tyabji, always ended with 'Bapu ki dua'.) By this, and by emphasizing monotheism, he was trying to bring together people of various faiths. He had recitations from different scriptures in his 'prayer' meetings; nevertheless, it was clear that he was a Hindu. But if Muslims were not to accept a devout Hindu as their leader, then does it not mean that they had already in their minds become separatists? Why should a devout Hindu leader be rejected by Muslims – a Hindu who is saying that they are like brothers to him, who is saying that the Muslims' religion is the Muslims' own business, who is saying that in the national wealth of India they would have an equal share? The real question is, why should Muslims feel that way? It is difficult to accept R.P. Dutt's position that because Gandhi said he was a devout Hindu, it alienated the Muslims. When Badshah Khan said he was a devout Muslim, it did not alienate the Hindus of the North-West Frontier. Muslim separatism did not arise, nor Hindu communalism, for the reason that Gandhi said that he was a devout Hindu. There are other reasons. True, as we have seen, there could be two paths to social reform: the religious framework of Gandhi and the totally secular framework of the Left. But the point is, we cannot judge between them today because it is the Gandhian path which succeeded; the Left was only marginally in competition in this area.

Now, I would take up two last questions. One is that of Quit India. I feel certain in my mind that Gandhi's decision to give the call of 'Quit India' then was a mistake. The Communist Party was quite right in opposing this resolution. It was clear that Gandhi's perception of the world at that time was not as clear as his perception of India. His actions clearly gave the impression that he thought the Allies were having a very hard time in the war, and therefore this was the time to get concessions. The Left too thought that the Allies were in a critical position, and therefore, if Soviet Russia was to be saved, this was the time to so conduct ourselves that all support could be given to the Allied cause. So we had the same perception of the world, but opposite inferences. The whole question is whether a temporary advantage for India was to guide the National Movement or the future of the world as a whole. These two opposite strategies were in conflict. Today we know that the Allies' position, though bad, was not so desperate as it appeared to Gandhi and his colleagues in the AICC, and to the Communist leadership. But this is the benefit of hindsight: Stalin was writing to Churchill and Roosevelt that Russia had lost so much territory that it could be defeated or be so weakened that it could no longer be of any assistance to the Allies. This was an extremely difficult time, between the offensive on Moscow and the battle of Stalingrad. There are surely times when the national interest comes into conflict with larger interests of the people of the world, and if the larger interest weighed with the Communist dissenters, I would, even at the present time when it is fashionable to regret it, hold it to be the right decision. I would also not condemn Gandhi for his position. The Indians had waited for far too long and had been patient. Gandhi had described the Extremists and the Moderates as the patient and the impatient lot, but patience had now run out for both. It became clear in the few succeeding months within 1942 that the Russian people and their Soviet system were strong enough to defeat Hitler, and the most stupendous battle in history, that of Stalingrad, was decisively won by the Red Army in the winter of 1942–43. This, ironically enough, had the immediate result that British imperialism did no longer need fear any great damage to its military cause by an Indian non-violent struggle and so did not need to talk with the imprisoned leaders.

My last point: I think Gandhi's 'finest hours' were the last months of his life. When communal massacres broke out upon Partition, Gandhi stood firmly by his principles; and here he could forget the narrow national interests for the larger cause. What he said could be distilled to this: 'I am as much concerned with the massacres in Pakistan as in India. But I must first stop the massacres in India; and therefore, I am going on fast here. When I succeed here, I would go for the same end to Pakistan, which is also my country.' For his fast, he made the additional demand that India must pay Rs 55 crore to Pakistan. For the Father of a Nation to take a direct position against his own nation, and in support of another country whose government was showering abuse on him day in and day out – this, I believe, was Gandhi's finest act. It was an action for which he ultimately gave his life at the hands of one of the heroes of the present Sangh Parivar. It seems to me that there is a message in this particular act for all serious political movements – the message that there is a point at which to compromise with principle is fatal. Gandhi's own success in stopping the massacres in India was achieved by frontally opposing the 'mainstream' perceptions. One must take a position that is right even if it is opposed to the national 'consensus'. How many of us could remember this in 1962 or 1965?

When we had a small war with Pakistan in 1965, our University held a meeting and our Chancellor said that if he had been young he would have gone to war alongside our jawans. Then we had a compromise at Tashkent and the same Chancellor, at a meeting held thereafter, told us it had been a very 'foolish war', and in effect quoted E.M.S. Namboodiripad. One realizes that in these national enthusiasms of the moment, particularly of the kind that we have had over Babri Masjid in 1992, and we will perhaps be going through such moments again and again, it is extremely important to take a principled position and to keep to it. I particularly wish to say that when

SAHMAT adopted a certain position in respect of Ayodhya, and when the Speaker defied all rules of the book to direct that the SAHMAT exhibition be removed from the premises of a public institution, it was a mark of honour for SAHMAT to be so favoured. What SAHMAT did was precisely in accordance with what Gandhiji had done; and therefore it is fitting today that while commemorating Safdar Hashmi, we are also celebrating Gandhi.

3

Jawaharlal Nehru's Historical Vision

It may seem presumptuous for a person like me, at best a professional historian, to take stock of a man of such greatness – a man of action, a man of intellect and of accomplishment – as Jawaharlal Nehru. But academic historians, as part of their profession, have to deal with great individuals, and they have the rare benefit of hindsight, which can supplement defeciences in their own intellectual calibre; and that must serve as my excuse for what I am doing now.

Jawaharlal Nehru was not only a maker of history, but also a writer of history. All the three major works that he wrote before Independence essentially dealt with history. There is another significant feature attaching to them: they were all written in prison. The first work, *Glimpses of World History*, was written in the form of letters, 96 of them, to a teenage daughter, Indira Gandhi, between 20 October 1930 and 9 August 1933, and published in 1934. During the time he was out of prison and when, finally, he was released, he no longer had any further time to

This is the text of a lecture, dedicated to the memory of Shri B.R. Nanda, that I was invited to deliver on the Foundation Day (28 April 2011) of the Nehru Memorial Museum and Library (NMML), New Delhi. I have revised the stenographic text kindly made available to me by NMML, and have added references to quotations. For the latter purpose it is essential to clarify that I have used the following editions of Nehru's three major works here considered: (1) *Glimpses of World History*, Jawaharlal Nehru Memorial Fund/Oxford University Press, New Delhi, 1982 (first impression); (2) *An Autobiography, with Musings on Recent Events in India*, The Bodley Head, London, reprinted with Additional Chapter, 1942; and (3) *The Discovery of India*, Meridian Books, London, 4th edition, 1956. I have often used the abbreviation *Glimpses* for (1) and *Discovery* for (3).

write any letter on history, except for an important postscript, dated 14 November 1938. His *Autobiography* was also similarly written in prison, from June 1934 to February 1935. *The Discovery of India* was written during his final period of imprisonment which extended from 9 August 1942 to 28 March 1945, the book being written within five months during 1944. These prison works invite comparison in both quantity and quality with the kind of writing that Antonio Gramsci produced as a Communist prisoner in fascist Italy. There are true similarities, in that both Gramsci and Nehru went to history in order to find answers to the questions that had been raised in their minds as men of action.

In all the three of his books, Jawaharlal Nehru disowns any claim to be a historian – I suppose, he means a professional historian. He claims that he wrote these books on the basis of 'odd books', on quotations taken down in note-books of his own over many years. In *Glimpses of World History*, he says he wanted to place his own country and himself in the context of a worldwide historical movement. As for the *Autobiography*, he wrote it almost in continuation of *Glimpses of World History*. Here he put his own life and experiences in the context of the Indian National Movement. He confesses in his 1936 Preface that his *Autobiography* is necessarily a 'wholly one-sided, and inevitably, egotistical' survey of the Indian National Movement ('recent Indian history'). Yet it is a major work on the National Movement, and has been used as a quarry by many historians. His *Discovery of India*, confessedly written to serve as a History of India, was written after a gap of ten years, and I will argue below that it came under a rather different impulse from the one behind his first two books.

In considering these three very important works, one must try to understand the intellectual method of Jawaharlal Nehru and the way he wished to see History. There are two ways of writing history, both of which are legitimate. In the first, one goes to one's sources, arranges the information one gets there in a rough logical or chronological order, and produces a narrative which simply describes what happened at a particular time in accordance with what the sources themselves describe. The second kind of history is different. In it one goes to the information collected in the same manner, but has certain questions to ask of this information. Those questions were not asked in the sources. The answers are only inferred from or built up by assembling the facts derived from the sources whose authors themselves were unconscious of the import of them for the modern questioner. A historical picture constructed from such an approach may be quite different from the picture that one would get from the first one.

Here ultimately one faces the kind of choice that Karl Marx framed in his theses on Feurbach in 1845: 'the philosophers have only *interpreted* the world in various ways. The point is to *change* it.' If building a future is the aim of one's study of the past, then history cannot consist of a directionless description. Nehru himself, in very plain words, expresses his distaste of conventional history, assembled from various pieces of information and arranged in a chronological order, with dates in abundance. (Nehru's distaste for dates did not, however, prevent him from painstakingly compiling a chronological table of world history, the only substantive addition to the *Glimpses*, besides the Postscript of 1938.) He is here actually expressing dissatisfaction with the first kind of history, the purely narrative one that I have mentioned. The second kind of history, in which one asks questions of it that persons of past ages never dreamt of, has to be really constructed out of the first kind, and that is precisely what Nehru does. What he achieves is not just a 'secondary work', but, in the words of a contemporary US reviewer (1934), 'one of the most remarkable books ever written' for its 'coherence and design' and 'breadth of culture' (this was said of the *Glimpses*). What Nehru's intellectual starting-point was at the time that he began to write *Glimpses of World History* in 1930, can be appreciated or recognized from his letters and other materials from that time, but his own *Glimpses* and his *Autobiography* give us ample understanding of it. Nehru felt a sense of deep dissatisfaction with the purpose of the National Movement, as a movement for Independence in merely constitutional terms. Gandhiji had expressed a similar dissatisfaction in 1909 in his *Hind Swaraj*. But Jawaharlal Nehru's source of dissatisfaction was different. What should happen after Independence was, to Nehru, not the restoration of the past as envisaged in Gandhiji's *Hind Swaraj*, but a modern India that was also to be a socialist society, where peasants would have land and where there would be public control of industry in the interest of the people; there would also be social reform, social liberation and, what he had particularly in mind, women's liberation.

Incidentally, I may say that references to facets of women's liberation (although the exact word 'liberation' is not used) are found scattered in all the three books. He quotes Lenin in *Glimpses*, p. 660, to the effect that 'no nation can be free when half of it is enslaved'. He expresses his indignation at many places at the *purdah* system and at attempts to keep women in seclusion; and one must remember that he was the draftsman of the Karachi Resolution of the Congress (1931) on Fundamental Rights, where a fully equal status as citizens was promised to women.

In other words, what Nehru is concerned with is the working out of how historical developments have taken place, and assessing thereby stages of human progress from the point of view not of the fortunate, but of the poor, the oppressed, the exploited, in order ultimately to understand how a situation could be brought about where they would be liberated.

So one goes to the past to work out the road for the present. In this quest, Nehru's own reading of Marxist classics contributed a great deal – he does not hide this indebtedness, nor does he proclaim it; it is simply assumed throughout, particularly in *Glimpses of World History* and in the *Autobiography*. In the *Autobiography*, he confesses: 'I incline more and more towards a communist philosophy' (p. 591). In the *Glimpses* (pp. 543–49) he provides a very sympathetic and accurate account of Marxism, but also touches on questions that he thinks are not fully answered in the framework of Marxism, quoting Lenin to the effect that Marxism is not something 'complete or unassailable'. Essentially, Marxism provides him with a starting-point; and it is no accident that he should point out that 1917, the year in which Indira Gandhi was born, was also the year of the Soviet Revolution, which he proclaimed as one of the major events in the history of mankind. He also names two particular persons whom he held to have eminently stood up for the cause of the poor, Lenin and Gandhi (*Glimpses*, p. 2).

Another element in his attitude towards history is an understanding that all people have contributed to historical development. They all have a place in it, and this raises a very interesting question in historiography. Is history to be democratized? That is to say, should historians study each class of people in a particular period according to the numbers of that class as if there is an adult suffrage or mass suffrage, in which the majority gets the greatest share of attention? Or should they deal mainly with persons and groups and classes who exercised the greatest influence on the historical movement? In the latter case, the masses appear only when, by their resort to resistance or agitation or by other developments, they contribute to the change or in any case affect the main course of events.

Though these alternatives are not posed by Nehru, his sympathies for the masses do not prevent him from writing history that is of the latter kind. On the one hand, he describes the impact of British colonial rule on the Indian poor where the influence of Karl Marx, Dadabhai Naoroji and Romesh Dutt is patent (e.g., *Glimpses,* pp. 416–25). On the other, he can admire the great creations of art, and is deeply interested in the way states of various kinds have arisen and fallen, in the emergence of different religions – and even in blood-thirsty conquerors. He has a long account of Changez Khan and wonders why that 'world-conqueror' 'should fascinate a peaceful and non-violent and mild person like me, who am ... a hater of everything feudal' (p. 220). So he takes in all strands of history, although his own standpoint is that of judging events from the point of view of the humanity at large. His history is far richer than a mere economic history or a narrative of the conditions of the common people, because he is also concerned with the processes of historical and cultural movements in which small classes and groups may play a far larger part than their numbers would justify. He can also see that all kinds of events intertwine. In a variant of the famous thesis in Karl Marx's article of 1853 on India about colonial Britain's unintended aid to India's regeneration, he could see that the British rulers objectively 'became the agents of a historical process in India – the process which was to change feudal India into the modern kind of industrialized capitalist state' (p. 419). History thus gets created by both the *elite* and the masses.

Another feature of the *Glimpses* which immediately invites respect is Nehru's concern with accuracy, though the works that he could consult were limited. He draws carefully from his note-books in which he had earlier taken notes from all kinds of sources. He confesses that there are many phases of world civilization that he had little information on at his disposal; he says in one of his letters that 'in a little paragraph in two or three short sentences I have disposed of Chinese history for 1000 years' (p. 28) – this in respect of a civilization which had such great achievements to its credit as the invention of paper, printing and gun-powder, and the holding of public service examinations. Nehru was thus aware that his account could not be as balanced as he wished. As he received information on something that he had missed out, he would return to that topic even when it was out of the chronological order. Thus, after reaching AD 1000, he goes back to the Indus valley civilization (pp. 186–88), because he had just been able to read in some detail about it. And yet the reader is conscious of always moving down with him as the whole of mankind evolved, created and struggled down the centuries. The accuracy of description is throughout remarkable. Apart from some misprints, the dates are carefully and correctly recorded. Despite his disparagement of the chronicle-kind of history, which I have already noted, he was well aware that time-markers are essential for establishing sequence, and thereby cause-and-effect.

A major feature of the *Glimpses* is that despite its title being suggestive of a fragmentary narrative, Nehru has the ambition here to embrace the whole of humanity – the Indian poor, as well as the Mayas of Mexico and Incas of Peru. He has also a very wide, almost comprehensive, perception of History. He is greatly interested in the transfer of Greek science to Arabs and how Arabs treated science, and he makes the remarkable statement that although the Greeks, Indians and others had scientific achievements to their credit, it was the Arabs who 'had this scientific spirit of enquiry, and so they may be considered the fathers of modern science' (p. 151). (By Arabs, he means the writers in the Arabic language in the early medieval period.) In the later portion of the book, his main concern shifts to capitalism as a world-wide system, the nature of colonialism as an offshoot of capitalism and the rise of Imperialism, of which his definition is not as narrow as that of Lenin. He probably did not know of Rosa Luxemburg's definition of it, but he realizes that imperialism emerges not only because of the conflict over world markets, but also because there is a maldistribution of wealth in capitalism which must result in over-production or under-consumption, creating thereby world-wide crises in which 'the law of the jungle' prevailed (pp. 353, 881ff). Capitalism thus led inevitably to imperialism.

The entire conclusion from his study of the historical process is that the inequities of capitalism can only be rectified by socialism (pp. 532ff). To Nehru, therefore, the Soviet Revolution of 1917 was of over-riding significance because it could show how socialism can work (pp. 645 ff and pp. 855–57). He did, however, enter caveats with regard to some aspects of Soviet life, especially in his 1938 postscript where he expressed concern at the trials in the late 1930s.

Besides the ills of capitalism, Nehru also points to certain other weaknesses in human civilizations. First of all, he expresses dissatisfaction with the way religion of all sorts limits and incapacitates the human mind. He mentions Hinduism, Buddhism, Christianity, Islam and other organized religions, and holds that they appeal to a wrong aspect of the human spirit, viz. the urge for after-life. In other words, they are not ethical enough. In the *Autobiography* he underlines this fact further, but in the *Glimpses* too, he cannot restrain himself from one very interesting remark, when he is dealing with Akbar – a remark that also shows how wide his reading was. He quotes a letter from Jesuit priests at Akbar's court in which the priests say of Akbar, 'thus we see in this Prince (King Akbar) the common fault of the atheist, who refuses to make reason subservient to faith'. Thereupon Nehru says, 'if this is the definition of an atheist, the more we have of them, the better' (p. 34). This not only constitutes praise for Akbar, but also a demand on the Indian people: that they too should leave aside faith and superstition, and pursue only reason and science – a call, in essence, for the total rejection of Traditional India.

The other phenomenon that disturbed Nehru was, rather unexpectedly, the emergence of nations and the break-up of humanity into territorially or racially self-serving groups. In his *Autobiography*, he holds the very concept of nation to be bourgeois; and anything bourgeois, in both *Glimpses of World History* and the *Autobiography*, calls for scornful rejection.

On the other hand, he believed that modern world-wide relationships were creating a new notion of humanity, linked to the cause of its progress. Indeed, the very 'idea of human progress is quite a modern notion' (*Glimpses*, p. 525). And after all, for Indian peasants and workers too 'nationalism and swaraj has no meaning unless it brings food and better conditions' (p. 505). I will argue presently that it is this outright rejection of religion and a critical reserve in respect of nationalism that set apart Nehru's first two books from his *Discovery of India*.

In *Glimpses of World History*, as also in the *Autobiography*, there are some remarkable historical insights of which I will give only two examples, one from *Glimpses* and the other from the *Autobiography*. I am thus anticipating my discussion of the *Autobiography*, but I regard these two as sister works where Nehru's ideas have not much changed. I have already drawn attention to Nehru's picking up a Jesuit condemnation of Akbar, in order to assert his own support of the cause of reason. It is pertinent to note that most historians (notably, V.A. Smith, in *Akbar the Great Mogul*, Oxford, 1917, which Nehru is likely to have seen or read) had hardly ever stressed Akbar's rationalist tendency, speaking only of his alleged new religion. It is only in recent years that Akbar's invocation of reason has received some attention, with Amartya Sen using it in a well-known article to deny the West's monopoly of the rational project. But I may add to this Nehru's comment on a much lesser figure. Of Mahmud of Ghazni, he says (*Glimpses*, p. 209) that 'in India he was prepared to kill "idolaters" with the help of Muslim soldiers; in Central Asia he was equally prepared to kill Muslims with the help of Hindu soldiers.' This succinct assessment, possibly based on facts given in Mohammad Habib's biography of Mahmud (1927), well anticipates Bosworth's work on Ghaznavids (1963) where he quotes a near-contemporary Persian source in which exactly this statement is made. This is just another instance of Nehru's unerring sense of cutting through irrelevant controversy in order to get at the essential historical fact. Such a sense, one is afraid, is not often given to a specialist of the profession.

Another insight I found most interesting is his statement in *Autobiography* where he discusses influences on India that entered with Islam. For reasons I do not know, he shows no recognition of Tara Chand's well-known work, *Influence of Islam on Indian Culture*, published in 1928, one of the notable contributions to Indian nationalist historiography of that time. Perhaps, he found its assumption that Islam, *as a religion*, was the fountainhead of important contributions to Indian culture, difficult to accommodate in his own strongly secular frame. He would rather attribute much of the cultural change to the Persian civilization, which continued to flower after Iran turned Muslim: 'But', he says, 'the influence of Persian [literature] has no element of religion about it. ... Persia was the France of the East, sending its language and culture to all its neighbours. This is a common and precious heritage for all of us in India' (*Autobiography*, p. 470). One wishes that some of the enthusiasts who are expelling Persian words from Hindi and Hindustani would read this particular statement of Jawaharlal Nehru, and appreciate how in the legacy of Persian literature, especially poetry, is embedded a culture of scepticism, nonconformity and defiance, a tradition which Nehru so aptly compared with what one has come to associate with France since the age of Enlightenment.

Glimpses of World History is very important today for another reason still. We are reminded from it that the barbaric acts of Imperialism have not changed. There is much in these letters about how British imperialism oppressed Egypt; and we can see from the *Glimpses* (pp. 773–77) how the US–British aggression against Iraq has had good precedent in British-ruled Iraq in the 1920s, when civilians there were also treated with 'late-bursting bombs' thrown on them from the air and with the 'gentle policy of destroying whole villages'. There is also much prescience in his criticism of British colonial policy in Palestine and the forcible implantation of Zionist settlements there (pp. 762–67). For Nehru, all those who opposed imperialism, whatever their hues, deserve admiration. It is good to remember that, for this reason, he has words of praise not only for Zaghlul Pasha, of the secular Egyptian Wafd, but also for Jamaluddin Afghani, the theorist of Pan-Islamism (pp. 583ff).

Glimpses of World History, therefore, is a work with a message. It is an ideological document of immense power because of its accuracy, because of its comprehensiveness and, above all, because of its sincerity. It served in its time as a very important ideological asset of our National Movement. But we will surely be poorer today too, if we forget or overlook its lessons from the past.

The *Autobiography* came soon after the *Glimpses,* written in Nehru's last term of imprisonment within the period of Civil Disobedience, and, in a sense, is practically a continuation of the history-writing project of which *Glimpses* was the first product. Titled *An Autobiography*, it is a far cry from a politician's self-justificatory text. It shares with Gandhiji's autobiographical *My Experiments with Truth* one feature only, which is that self-criticism, rather than self-serving narration, is its dominant element. But it is only partly a biography: as Nehru himself admits, it looks like 'a survey of recent Indian history'; but it is a survey in which the questions and problems facing India and the National Movement, as seen by Nehru himself, take centre-stage. Nehru's own life story is subordinated to that larger historical narration, one which may be 'one-sided', in the view of some, but is never 'egotistical', even if that is what Nehru himself says. What is singular about this 'survey' is that no one before had subjected the history of our National Movement to such a rational analysis, especially one in which the Marxist sociological method is also employed. Yet there is here no straitjacketed interpretation: Nehru is far too conscious of variations in historical contexts to pass any black-and-white judgements on people with whom he differed. Thus he is not scornful of the early moderates, however scornful he might be of his 'moderate' contemporaries. He realizes that it was they who pioneered a tangible, anti-colonial theoretical framework. The writings of Dadhabhai Naoroji, R.C. Dutt and William Digby, he says, 'in spite of the moderate outlook of their authors, served a revolutionary purpose and gave a political and economic foundation to our nationalism' (p. 426): the Indian people now knew what they were fighting against and why. On the other hand, despite his admiration for the boldness or bravery of those who at that time espoused 'extremism', Nehru cannot conceal his disagreement with their revivalist aims. His own position about the implications of the gains of the 'Extremists' during the early years of the twentieth century were clearly stated thus:

> Socially speaking, the revival of India's nationalism in 1907 was definitely reactionary. Inevitably, a new nationalism in India, as elsewhere in the East, was a religious nationalism. The Moderates ... [in comparison] represented a more advanced social outlook, but they were a mere handful on the top side with no touch with the masses. (p. 24)

In other words, only those in that early stage could mobilize large numbers on the nationalist side who could invoke the support of religion.

Nehru constantly felt called upon to ponder on the divisive and reactionary force that religion represented in the national movement as well as generally in human affairs: 'The spectacle of what is called religion, or at any rate organized religion, in India and elsewhere has filled me with horror. I have frequently condemned it and wished to make a clean sweep of it' (p. 374). On an argumentative plane, he conceded in words that remind us of Marx's formula about religion being 'the opium of the people': religions, says Nehru, 'offer a safe anchorage from doubt and mental conflict in assurance of a future life' (p. 376). For himself he rejected such a 'harbourage'; but what of the impact of religion on the people at large and the fight for freedom?

In India these religious influences took their shape in what came to be called communalism, which, next to British power, seemed to have become the greatest obstacle to the National Movement. Nehru's own basic aim was, of course, the one he had already put in *Glimpses* (p. 234): 'We must put an end to it [Hindu–Muslim bitterness] ... But what is important is to get out of the complex ideology of custom, convention and superstition, which under the guise of religion enchains us.' But the very complexity of communalism demanded a careful analysis of it, which indeed he proceeds to provide in the *Autobiography* in an entire chapter devoted to communalism (pp. 458–72).

Here, an important point that had already been made in the *Glimpses* is now repeated: the ability of Hindu communalism to masquerade as Indian nationalism, whereas it was easier to identify Muslim communalism for what it was (*Glimpses*, p. 720; *Autobiography*, p. 467). Nehru tests both these communalisms by their willingness to submit to British rule, and support for all the conservative and exploitative elements in India. In a very perceptive assessment of Sir Syed Ahmad Khan, he could not hold back from underlining the irony of that educationist supporting 'our aristocracy' against men 'of low-caste or insignificant origin', quite forgetful of the claims made on behalf of 'the democracy of Islam' (p. 463). His ire falls equally on Madan Mohan Malaviya (pp. 458–59). If Gandhiji had agreed in *Hind Swaraj* that the nation had nothing to do with religion, Nehru goes on to argue that culture too cannot be identified with any religion (p. 471). This, of course, meant that Nehru was also rejecting much of the legacy of our past –

'the harmful' part of it, as he says, that backward-looking Hindus and Muslims were always 'clutching at' (ibid.).

The *Autobiography* is also important for much factual evidence – notably of the 'qualitative' kind – about the National Movement that it provides, often of a kind that cannot be gained from either browsing in the archives or compiling statistics, although these too are essential. To give one instance: in the early days of 1931 Nehru accompanied Gandhi-ji to Delhi, at the time of negotiations leading to the Gandhi–Irwin Agreement. He tells us (p. 251):

> A ceaseless stream of people, of high and low degree, came to Dr. Ansari's house, where Gandhiji and most of us were staying, and in our leisure moments, we watched them with interest and profit. For some years our chief contacts had been with the poor in towns and villages and those who were down and out in jails. The very prosperous gentleman who [now] came to visit Gandhiji showed us another side of human nature and a very adaptable side, for wherever they sensed power and success, they turned to it and welcomed it with the sunshine of their smiles. Many of them were staunch pillars of the British Government in India. It was comfortable to know that they would become equally staunch pillars of any other government that might flourish in India.

Such an observation of human nature cannot come from dry official documents.

Now, when one thinks of events after 1947, and of ICS and IPS officers arresting A.K. Gopalan and others for undermining the authority of His Majesty the King during the time we were still a Dominion (1947–50), with the same vigour with which they had arrested Congress leaders in the 1930s and early 1940s, one should surely recall this passage. We also saw how after 1947, princes became Members of Parliament and turned into Congress leaders with perfect ease. I do not know if Pandit Nehru himself at any time recollected the passage that I have just quoted. But if he did, while he watched this rapid acceptance of the new regime by such eminent and elegant loyalists of yesteryear, he doubtless must have smiled.

One need not here spend much space to recall Nehru's affection and regard for Gandhiji, as also his assessment of the historical role of that very great man: 'The little fact remains that this "reactionary" [Nehru is here referring to hostile Leftist appraisals of Gandhiji] knows India, understands India, almost *is* peasant India and has shaken up India as no so-called revolutionary has done. Even his latest Harijan activities have gently but irresistibly undermined orthodox Hinduism and shaken it to its foundations' (p. 406). Yet, despite such admiration, Nehru does not hold Gandhiji to be above criticism.

He says (pp. 255–56) that he had thought earlier that he could influence Gandhiji to move 'in a socialist direction'; but he realized now [1935?] that 'there are basic differences between Gandhiji's ideals and the socialist objective'. This distance between his own goals and those of Gandhiji could only increase because 'Gandhiji did not encourage others to think' (p. 373), and exercised a 'psychic coercion ... which reduces many of his intimate followers to a state of mental pulp' (p. 539). He claims that Gandhiji took decisions without consultation ('his old dictatorial self' – p. 554). He was concerned with the way Gandhiji had withdrawn the Non-Cooperation Movement in 1922 (see p. 81) and even more so with the suspension of Civil Disobedience under the Gandhi–Irwin Agreement of 1931 ('a great emptiness as of something gone, almost beyond recall', p. 259). It was not only, however, a matter of discomfort with certain tactical, even strategic decisions taken by Gandhiji. The issues stemmed from a basic disagreement: Nehru says that he shares the criticisms of others, who were disturbed about Gandhiji's inclination towards metaphysics (p. 304), which naturally discouraged rationality. But the differences encompassed essentially the attitude to be taken towards the idle and the exploiting classes.

Thus Nehru has bitter words for what he considered Gandhiji's tendency to grant concessions to the princes. He himself had no use for the princes. He points out that when C.R. Das was very ill, the Dogra ruler of Kashmir would not allow him to enter Kashmir though he had reached its border; and when Jinnah was still committed to Home Rule, the Nizam of Hyderabad did not allow him to enter Hyderabad (p. 532). These acts showed how the princes were shamelessly loyal to the British government. After all they were autocrats created by the British government for its own purposes and maintained by it. He was therefore greatly agitated at the fact that Gandhiji had 'fathered a novel policy on the Congress', that of 'non-interference in affairs' of the states. He points out that in 1934, in his letter to N.C. Kelkar, the President of the State Subjects Conference, Gandhiji had gone so far as to claim that the states are 'independent entities under British law (!)' and so immune from interference from people of 'British India' (see *Autobiography*, pp. 531–32).

Similarly, Nehru takes great exception to Gandhiji's assurances to the big zamindars of U.P., given also in 1934, that their property would not be taken away and that if anyone tried to do so, 'you will find me fighting on your side' (p. 535). Nehru complains that under this impulse, the Congress Working Committee began to go back on the promises that had been made to the Indian people in the Fundamental Rights Resolution at the Karachi Congress in 1931 (p. 557). He himself was well aware that the Fundamental Rights Resolution was not socialist in content, and even suggested that 'a capitalist state could easily accept everything contained in the resolution' (p. 266). But even so, the fact that the Congress Working Committee's resolutions should actually seek to diminish the value of the rights promised to the peasants and workers, and should do so with Gandhiji's blessings, had naturally a 'painful effect' on Nehru, who was still in jail (p. 557).

When one reads these statements in the *Autobiography*, published for all to see, one is impressed immediately with one fact: the greatness of the two men, both Gandhi and Nehru, in that they should continue to dispute and disagree publicly with each other, while combining together in a remarkable partnership against British Imperialism. Nehru says his vision of India was quite different from that of Gandhiji; yet the eminent needs of the struggle for freedom demanded not simply an alliance, but a deeply personal association.

Nehru, as we have noted, speaks of his illusion that he could persuade Gandhiji to take a socialist direction. But would the circumstances and needs of the partnership with Gandhiji in time influence Nehru's own larger vision? A careful reader would note important points of difference of attitude between the *Glimpses of World History* and the *Autobiography*, on one side, and the *Discovery of India*, on the other; and one should examine why this is so.

In the *Glimpses* and the *Autobiography*, Nehru regards the concept

of nation itself as bourgeois. He recognized, while speaking of 'orthodox Communists', that 'many of their theoretical criticisms of Congress ideology were able and pointed'; and some of their 'analyses of
the general Indian situation turned out to be remarkably correct'.
Their essential error lay rather in forgetting that the Indian National
Movement was not 'a labour or proletarian movement'. 'It is a *bourgeois* movement as its very name ["national"] implies' (*Autobiography*, pp. 365–66). In other words, only a bourgeois democratic state
(i.e. a capitalist state) could be expected to result from the National
Movement.

True, these statements belonged to the period before the Communist movement (of which Nehru was at least an interested observer)
developed its concept of Popular Front, formalized at the Comintern's
7th Congress, 1935. One could now regard the Indian National Movement as a coalition of classes; but this was not the position that Nehru
was familiar with when composing his *Autobiography*. We must remember that in the *Glimpses* he had already said that the concept of
'nation' implied a division of humanity. The National Movement was
necessary because Imperialism needed to be overthrown and that could
only be done nationally. So the inherent limitations of the National
Movement must be borne in mind. He recognized that India had had
a great culture in the past in some respects, but there had been evils
too, and now modern values, rationalism, social equality, etc., needed
to prevail, and Indians must learn to make a break with their past
culture in major matters involving economic and social institutions.
He even noted, as we have seen, that he felt inclined 'more and more
towards a communist philosophy', though he could not accept any
text as scripture (*Autobiography*, p. 591). But these ideas do not at all
maintain their centrality and, to some extent, even presence, in the
Discovery of India; and one must search for an explanation.

In 1940, in a Postscript to his *Autobiography*, written after World
War I had broken out, Nehru was sure on what side he was in respect to
Nazi Germany, despite his hostility to the British government which
he continued to express in this text. 'The challenge of fascism and
nazism was in essence the challenge of imperialism', he said. Since
'the problem of India was tied with world problems' (p. 601), it was
clear on which side India must stand. Nehru clearly shows his dismay

at the fascist powers' successes in the war. He had a premonition, perhaps, of things to come when, in his 1938 postscript to the *Glimpses*, he said that the fascist threat could only be met when Soviet Russia and the US entered the struggle (*Glimpses*, p. 971). In 1941, this very situation came about from the aggressive actions of the fascist powers themselves. In June Germany attacked the Soviet Union, and in December Japan bombed Pearl Harbour. Contrary to Nehru's hopes of 1938, even US military experts gave the Soviet Union at best six months before the inevitable collapse. China, in whose cause Nehru had special interest (*Autobiography*, p. 608), was nearly over-run by Japan. Faced with such a crisis, when there was an imminent threat of the triumph of naked racialism and barbarism, elementary international solidarity demanded that the primary duty of all was to ensure that Germany and Japan were defeated. This followed from the logic of Nehru's own statements, which were, of course, far more numerous on this count than I have quoted.

A problem that faced India in responding to this call was the attitude of the British Government: no crisis in the War would be allowed to slacken its control over India (*Autobiography*, Postscript, pp. 608–09). Even when Burma had fallen, Cripps' Proposals, in early 1942, were of such a kind that these could not be accepted by the Congress.

Now, I do not know what course Nehru himself expected the National Movement to take. He probably thought that the Congress would continue to differ with the British Government, but not allow itself to call for any direct struggle against it. He confesses in the *Discovery* that he and some like-minded people became 'disturbed and upset' at the uncompromising position ('based on a narrow view of nationalism') that Gandhiji began taking against the British Government in 1942, which created tremendous excitement in the country (p. 483). We now know that Gandhiji even asked Nehru in a letter to resign from the Working Committee if he did not agree to the course of decisions which ultimately led to the Quit India Resolution of 7 and 8 August 1942. On his part, Nehru says plainly in the *Discovery* that 'in a conflict between the two, nationalism had triumphed over internationalism' (p. 483). The causes on the world scale that he had supported in *Glimpses of World History* and in *Autobiography* now stood contradicted by the basic assumptions of the Quit India Resolution

and its substantive defiance of Indian people's international obliga-
tion, despite lip-service to the Allied cause. But at the end of it all, the
fact remained that Nehru went along with it, and was as much committed to the Quit India Resolution after 8 August as anyone else.
Along with other Congress leaders he too was arrested on 9 August.

I submit that the *Discovery of India* has to be seen in the light of this
shift in Nehru's position against all the dictates of convictions that he
had held up till now. The first result is that not the world, but India
becomes his focus.

At the end of his introductory chapter of the book (p. 24) Nehru
quotes, apparently as the starting-point of his survey of India, the statement Gandhiji made on 8 August 1941, to the effect that 'we must
look the world in the face with calm and clear eyes even though the
eyes of the world are bloodshot today'. Surely, this was an unkind statement on behalf of India to a world fighting for survival and elementary
dignity, at a time when the battle of Stalingrad was deciding the fate of
Soviet Russia and the Chinese people were shedding their blood to
save the residual territory left to them. What had the people of the
world done to us? Why should India look at the world in the face? It is
difficult to understand why, of all persons, Jawaharlal Nehru, should
have picked these words of Gandhiji as worth remembering, recording
thereby his own endorsement of them.

Perhaps, he felt that there was now the need to justify India to the
world. If so, it may be valid to argue that the *Discovery of India* has been
constructed in a large part to offer such a justification, while continuing – and that is important too – within at least part of the framework
that Nehru had already framed for his historical interpretations in
Glimpses and *Autobiography*. Yet one notices the sharp change from
internationalism to nationalism. Now Nehru even draws some com-
fort (p. 529) from the concessions made by the Soviet leaders to Russian nationalism at a very critical juncture during the War, when they
wanted allies of every sort. That could not surely be a blanket justification for narrow nationalism, particularly when the desperate situation
in which Soviet Union found itself was an adequate explanation for
the appeal to national sentiment, even to Slav solidarity, which appealed to not only national but even ethnic sentiment.

As far as India is concerned, it is suddenly elevated to a much higher position than it occupies in the *Glimpses of World History* and *Autobiography*. Nehru agrees – and that is why the framework is preserved, but the emphasis is elsewhere – that India must break with much of her past and not allow the past 'to dominate the present' (p. 522). But soon it is followed by this astounding assertion: 'We can never forget the ideals that have moved our race.' What ideals (the caste system, religion?) have 'moved our race'? Was social equality, women's freedom, ever part of our culture, rife otherwise with caste and religious prejudices? Is it that if we 'forget them or cease to take pride in that noble heritage ... [there] will no longer remain India', as Nehru now asserts (p. 522)? It seems to reverse, or at least qualify substantively, whatever Nehru had said in his two earlier works. Contrary to the hostility to organized religion shown in those works, now there is the unqualified – and surely, historically unprovable – declaration that 'religions have helped greatly in the development of humanity' (p. 524). There is, it is true, still a flash of the old in the statement: 'Even if God exists, it may be desirable not to look up to Him, or rely upon Him' (p. 526). But even this is diluted elsewhere: after acknowledging that some of his earlier ideals had lost their lustre (p. 11), this loss of their shine allows him now to admit that there could be a soul, and, given this assumption, 'there appears to be some logic also in the theory of reincarnation' (p. 13). Even after confessing that he himself is not interested in after-life, he concedes that he 'can appreciate to some extent the conception of monism, and I have been attracted towards the Advaita (non-dualist) philosophy of the Vedanta ... but minus the conception of God or Gods' (p. 14).

No one will disagree that the theory of transmigration of souls found in the Upanishads, and in Jainism and Buddhism, has been an important element of ancient Indian thought; and so has been pantheism, particularly as set forth by Shankaracharya. These speculations are part of our heritage, and they need to be given due importance even by those who do not believe in them. But Jawaharlal Nehru now assigns to such thought a toweringly high position, so that it seems as if since the moment of their enunciation there has only been a descent: 'One senses a progressive deterioration during centuries. The urge to life and endeavour becomes less, the creative spirit fades away and gives place to the imitative' (p. 41). This contrast between the creative and imitative elements in any civilization is surely highly problematical, since a society which does not constantly learn from outside in matters of techniques, ideas and knowledge is not likely to be very creative.

Here, one has necessarily to mention Nehru's willingness to accept the unhistorical frame in which Sir Sarvepalli Radhakrishnan set Indian philosophy. It was ironical, of course, for the knight-philosopher, himself on such good terms with the foreign rulers, to say that (in Nehru's words) 'Indian philosophy lost its vigour with the loss of political freedom' (p. 218). Nehru unfortunately contests not the notion, but the cause: India lost its political freedom because there was internal decay during these thousand years [first millennium AD]' (p. 218). Such a view may justifiably lead the reader to think that medieval India formed India's Dark Ages, though one would like to feel that Nehru would not himself have drawn such an inference.

These features about the *Discovery of India* are, indeed, disturbing. But there is another side too. Who can say that India and its history do not constitute a worthy subject? If there is a retreat from the uncompromisingly rational position of the *Glimpses* and *Autobiography*, even an admission, in effect, of the triumph of nationalism over internationalism in Nehru's own thought (*Discovery*, p. 40), many elements of the earlier works still shine through: the wide reading, the same broad range of narrative, the same anxiety for accuracy (factual slips are few). There are insights spread throughout, like observing that in the Jat and Satnami uprisings of the seventeenth century, the poor were for the first time entering the business of revolts: he quotes a Mughal source (drawn from Jadunath Sarkar?), but his insight has precedence over W.C. Smith's seminal article on these 'lower-class' revolts, published in 1946. There is a constant endorsement of the evolution of a common (composite) culture. And there is a very persuasive chapter on the question of Muslims and the Muslim League, which would especially bear reading today (pp. 385–400).

I may close with a reference to what I found fifty years ago (1961) when I was asked to participate in a symposium on Historians and National Integration, under the auspices of the Indian History Congress. After some search, the one book on Indian history I could recommend from that point of view was Nehru's *Discovery of India*. The *Discovery* is a text on history in which all sections of our people would find something of their past, a good reason surely why even today this book should be celebrated. But this is not to say that any book that is celebrated does not have certain points of dispute. In a sense, a reader has to choose between the author of the *Glimpses* and the *Autobiography*, and the author of the *Discovery of India*, the first two written when the ideals were bright, the last when those ideals had dimmed somewhat (by Nehru's own admission). But surely, whatever choice we make, the entire trilogy will remain a very precious part of our intellectual heritage.

4

Civil Disobedience, 1930–31

British imperialism's position – after its triumph in 1918 over its main challenger, Germany, and the largely successful containment of Soviet Russia – was now reinforced in India by the embarrassingly abrupt withdrawal of the Non-Cooperation Movement in February 1922. The Union Jack seemed unassailably ascendant over the 'Indian Empire', with the nationalists forced into a demoralized and disorderly retreat. A division in the nationalist camp erupted between the Gandhian 'No-Changers' sticking to individual non-cooperation and the 'Swarajist' proponents of electoral participation as a means of carrying on political opposition to the government. When, in 1926, the Swarajists experienced severe reverses in the elections, compared with their 1923 performance, the 'Responsivists', seeking to become ministers under the Dyarchy, began to split the Swarajist camp as well. Simultaneously, the Hindu–Muslim chasm grew as the Hindu critics of nationalism's espousal of Khilafat, on the one hand, and Muslim leaders' outcry against its alleged betrayal of the same Khilafat, on the other, undermined the platform of communal unity that Non-Cooperation in 1920–22 had so splendidly built up. Gandhi's fast in 1924 in protest against the growth of communalism had only limited effect; 1925 saw the establishment of the RSS, and Swami Shraddhanand's murder. Well could Lord Birkenhead, the Secretary of State for India, claim in 1925, that 'the unsubstantial ghost of nationalism' was being laid to rest.

This article was originally written for SAHMAT's publication, *Indian People in the Struggle for Freedom*, New Delhi, 1998.

The British Government accordingly felt that this was the best time for it to institute a constitutional review that would place the nationalists further in their place. The Government of India Act, 1919, had provided for the appointment, after ten years, of a statutory commission to recommend, after scrutiny, whether 'to extend, modify or restrict the degree of [existing] responsible government'.[1] The appointment of this commission was now advanced by two years, and on 8 November 1927 the announcement was made of the commission that was to be headed by the 'liberal', Sir John Simon. India's fate could now be determined firmly by seven men representing the different components of the Imperial establishment,[2] while the Indians bickered and quarrelled among themselves.

In the event, the step proved to be a gross miscalculation, turning out to be a provocation rather than a coup. This was because its authors ignored the basic reality that despite nationalism's recent discomfitures, two fundamental factors had not changed, namely, India's continuing impoverishment under British rule, and the Indian people's urge for freedom.

What else could represent the continuing poverty of India more dramatically than the average expectation of life at birth, estimated at less than 25 years over the decade 1921–31; it had practically remained stagnant since four decades earlier (1881–91), when it was 25.5 years.[3] Only 9 per cent of the population was returned as literate in 1931, which reflected the acute cultural backwardness from which India suffered after some 150 years of British rule. Each sector of the Indian economy was under pressure. The Royal Commission on Indian Agriculture, reporting in 1928, drew a sombre picture of land-exhaustion, for which it could offer only trivial remedies, a prudent government having placed outside the scope of its enquiries the two major drains on the peasant's essential resources, viz. rent and taxation. At the same time the 1931 census found only one Indian out of nine living in the towns, showing how little employment outside agriculture was available. A 'free trade' policy had been relentlessly followed to throttle Indian industry in the interests of imports from Britain. The 1923 Fiscal Commission's scheme of 'discriminating protection' (with which all its Indian members dissented) left the bulk of the Indian industrial sector unprotected. In order further to encourage British imports, the rupee was statutorily pegged at 1s.6d. (up from 1s.4d.) in 1927. Every class of Indians, except, perhaps, the large land-owners, had reason to nurse deep-seated grievances, which no constitutional jugglery could sweep away.

It was not only that the ground for the grievances existed: political consciousness was also spreading at different levels and in divergent forms, which necessarily undermined and restricted the authority commanded by the loyalist and collaborationist camps. First of all, after his release from prison in February 1924, Gandhi had thrown himself body and soul into the pursuit of his 'Constructive Programme', concentrating on 'Swadeshi', especially through the promotion of *khadi* (hand-spun and hand-woven cloth), Hindu–Muslim unity and the removal of untouchability; he also preached temperance and the need for spreading education. His major objective was the villages, and he combined extensive tours with careful organizational work, building up bodies such as the Khadi Board. By 1928 he had built up a network of centres and volunteers throughout India, giving him practical access to hundreds of thousands of the rural poor. In the North-West Frontier Province (NWFP), Khan Abdul Ghaffar Khan, braving intermittent imprisonments, built up an educational and social movement among the Pathans, centred round the Pakhtoon Jirga, established in 1926; it would soon become a vanguard component of the Indian national movement.

The Swarajist appeal lay more among the educated middle classes despite their late leader C.R. Das's (d. 1925) declared commitment to 'the 98 per cent'. But their continuous and often able opposition to the British government in the central legislative assembly (where even after 1926 they held 38 out of the 100 elected seats) and provincial councils constantly projected the nationalist case to everyone who read newspapers.

Beyond these two major components of the Congress camp, there was beginning to come into the scene a new current, admittedly affected by the resolute opposition to imperialism by Soviet Russia, and the practical illustration it gave to the liberation of workers and peasants under socialism. Its most prominent exponent was Jawaharlal Nehru, son of the Swarajist leader Motilal Nehru. In December 1927, at the Congress session at Madras, having 'recently arrived from Russia, [he] addressed the delegates as "comrades"'.[4] He also moved a resolution which was duly passed, much to the chagrin of the established leaders, declaring that 'the goal of the Indian people was complete national independence'. With Subhas Chandra Bose, he had just established the Independence for India League to organize radical youth for the cause.

Under the new socialist impulse there was a reorientation of the revolutionary nationalist groups as well, who were trying to recover from the Kakori Conspiracy Case (following upon the train attack at Kakori on 8 August 1925), in which four revolutionaries (Ashfaqullah, Bismil, Roshan Singh and Lahiri) were hanged, and twenty-one others sentenced to life and long-term imprisonments. In March 1926 Bhagat Singh founded the Naujiwan Bharat Sabha, with the aim of establishing 'a republic of labourers and peasants'. He and Chandrashekhar Azad were to reorganize the old Hindustan Republican Army (H.R.A.) as the Hindustan Socialist Republican Army (H.S.R.A.) in September 1928, in a secret meeting at Delhi.

Soviet and socialist influences were, of course, most directly the source of inspiration for the Communists. Constantly harassed by the police – four of their leaders were sentenced to four years' imprisonment in the Kanpur Conspiracy Case (1924) – the Communists still succeeded in establishing the Workers' and Peasants' Party in the main provinces, and becoming an influential militant force in the trade unions.

II

Without the often silent impact of these various currents within the national movement, it is not possible to explain why the Viceroy, Lord Irwin's confident boast in May 1927 of being 'able to break the boycott of the Hindu Congress' of the projected Simon Commission proved such an empty one. He would only now discover that the Indian national sensitivities had reached such a point that a commission due to report to the British Parliament was not acceptable, even for preliminary negotiations, simply because it was all-white and contained no Indian.

A constitutional war has been declared on Great Britain. Negotiations are not to come from our side. Let the Government sue for peace. We are denied equal partnership. We will resist the new doctrine to the best of our power. Jallianwallah Bagh was a physical butchery, the Simon Commission is a butchery of our souls. By appointing an exclusively white Commission, Lord Birkenhead has declared our unfitness for self-government. ...[5]

These words came not from Jawaharlal Nehru, but Mohammad Ali Jinnah, at the Muslim League's Calcutta session on 1 January 1928, as he declared his support for the national boycott of the Simon Commission. In this boycott the Congress was also joined by the Liberals and the Hindu Mahasabha. In February, even the Central Assembly carried a motion expressing 'lack of confidence' in the Simon Commission: the vote was 68 to 62 in a house where nearly a third of the members were officials or government nominees.

It was not only that practically every leader with any large following refused to rise to the bait of giving 'evidence' before the Commission. For the first time since the end of Non-Cooperation, there developed a nation-wide agitation. An all-India *hartal* was organized on 3 February 1929 when the Commission landed at Bombay, and protest demonstrations (usually with black flags and the slogan 'Simon Go Back') and local *hartal*s were witnessed at every place subsequently visited by the Commission in its journey in India. This was notwithstanding an unrestrained degree of police repression: when the Commission arrived at Lahore on 30 October, a huge procession, led by the redoubtable Lala Lajpat Rai, was attacked by the police, and, himself gravely injured, he died on 17 November.

The political agitation was accompanied by a new militancy in the working class. Official returns indicated a jump in the number of working days lost due to 'disputes' from a mere 2.0 million in 1927 to 31.6 million in 1928. Some 1,50,000 Bombay textile workers remained on strike from April to October 1928, ultimately winning many of their demands through the government-appointed Fawcett Committee. Leadership in these struggles almost completely passed from the hands of the non-political trade unionists into those of the Communists.

Peasant stirrings were similarly being harnessed by Gandhi's khadi-clad army. The centre-stage in this was occupied by the Bardoli Satya-graha, undertaken in a district of Gujarat against revenue enhance-ments imposed after a new settlement. Led by Vallabhbhai Patel, the peasants, from February 1928 onwards, refused to pay the enhanced revenue and braved forfeitures; by August they had forced the govern-ment practically to capitulate. The importance of the Bardoli agitation is defined, not necessarily lessened, by the fact that it was essentially one of peasant-proprietors ('*pattidars*'), not peasant-tenants. The national attention it received was richly deserved, since it foreshadow-ed the future massive entry of the peasants into the Civil Disobedience Movement.

The revolutionaries made their own mark on the political scene when Bhagat Singh and his comrades shot dead an English police offi-cer on 17 December 1927, to avenge the death of Lala Lajpat Rai. For long the authors remained undetected.

Both to sustain the momentum of the nationalist agitation and to consolidate the alliance with the other groups that had come together in opposing the Simon Commission, it was imperative to present a united platform of what 'Political India' (a favourite expression of those days) wanted. Accordingly, an all-parties conference met in Delhi at the call of the Congress on 12 February 1928, with a second session at Bombay on 19 May; a report on what India's constitution should be was prepared by a committee headed by Motilal Nehru, and this was approved at the all-parties conference at Lucknow in late August. The report was moderate in asking only for 'dominion status', of the same type as possessed by the white dominions. The Muslims were to be given reservation of seats in joint electorates in provinces where they were in a minority; the electorate was to be based on universal adult suffrage; and the provinces were to have autonomy in specified spheres. In late December the all-parties convention met at Calcutta to con-sider the detailed provisions.

It was here unfortunately that, by what now seems to have been a tactical error by the Congress leadership, the alliance suffered a set-back. Jinnah proposed five points, among which the most important were the raising of Muslim representation in the central legislature from 27 per cent to 33.3 per cent, and a federation with residuary powers vested in the provinces. By siding with the Hindu Mahasabha in rejecting all the five points, the convention seemingly helped to fulfil Birkenhead's objective of leaving 'Jinnah high and dry'.[6] Gandhi, anxious to present the fruits of the all-parties' labours to the Congress session, meeting almost simultaneously at Calcutta, for once abstained from the role of a peace-maker. Scornful of such wrangles, Jawaharlal Nehru in his *Autobiography* passes over the episode in silence.[7] The latter's view-point was shared by the Communists speaking through the Workers and Peasants Party, which, while accepting 'the solution proposed to the communal question' by the All-parties' Report, argued that the question hardly merited such an 'excessive amount of attention' since 'experience tends to show that there is little communal feeling among the masses'.[8] This can now be recognized as a wishful downgrading of the ideological factor in the name of simple economism or idealistic nationalism. One can only agree with the official history of the freedom movement, that such an attitude at this time, leading to a 'parting of the ways' with a very influential section of the Muslim leadership, created a persistent division among the people, which imperialism was henceforth so gleefully to exploit.[9]

For the moment, however, the major controversy in the Congress session at Calcutta was over whether to compromise over dominion status or go forward to a struggle for independence directly. The matter was of more than academic interest, because the recommendations of the All-parties' Report were so drafted that control over the armed forces and foreign affairs could possibly continue with Britain.[10] The two sides were so evenly matched in the Congress that Gandhi compromised by moving a resolution (31 December 1928) that the offer to accept Dominion Status stood only if the British Government accepted the All-parties' Report by the end of 1929; if it failed to do so, Non-Cooperation would be the next resort and total independence the aim. Even so, Subhas Bose's amendment contesting the compromise on dominion status gathered 973 votes (including Jawaharlal's), with 1,350 against.

It might not have been clear in Calcutta on that day, but Gandhi's compromise resolution, by conceding that no agitation would be launched for the All-parties' Report, left it all but politically dead. For all practical purposes, Gandhi himself was now committed to the goal of complete independence (Purna Swaraj), which, with his instinctive espousal of tactically moderate slogans, was an enormous concession to the radicals.

III

The Calcutta Congress resolution, while it served a defiant notice on imperialism, also gave it a year's respite. The British Government sought to use this period to deprive the Congress of its existing allies, by repression as well as blandishments.

First came the turn of the Communists. Their growing strength had been displayed by a procession of some 20,000 red-flag-waving mill-hands of Calcutta, who, before the inception of the Calcutta session of the Congress, had occupied the *pandal* for nearly two hours, demanding that it should accept the goal of complete independence. On 21 February 1929, the Government of India addressed a policy letter to the provincial governments voicing the suspicion that 'Congressmen like Jawaharlal Nehru' might enter into 'temporary alliance with Communists, who had been active among the industrial workers of Calcutta and Bombay'.[11] The very next month, in a sudden sweep, the Government arrested thirty-one Communist and labour leaders (with one more arrested later) in various parts of the country, charging them with conspiracy 'to deprive the King of the sovereignty of British India'. They were brought to Meerut (U.P.) for trial ('Meerut Conspiracy Case') and remained prisoners as undertrials until January 1933, when heavy sentences were imposed, Muzaffar Ahmad receiving one of transportation for life. In April 1929 the Government re-introduced a Public Safety Bill in the central legislature to arm itself with more powers. Accompanying this was much official propaganda about Russian gold and 'Bolshevik' conspiracy.

Had the Congress leadership faltered and joined in the clamour against the Communists, the Government might have gained political mileage by appearing as a defender of law and order in India. But Congress leaders of even a moderate complexion spiritedly denounced the Government's actions, immediately forming a defence committee for the Meerut accused, with Motilal Nehru as chairman and Dr M.A. Ansari and Jawaharlal Nehru as members. How 'non-cooperation from within' could take place within the legislature was illustrated not only by the stout opposition to the Public Safety Bill in the central assembly, but also, remarkably, by the Assembly president Vitthalbhai Patel's refusal to allow a discussion of the Bill since it could prejudice the defence of the Meerut accused, and, then, by his use of his casting vote to defeat the Bill. The Viceroy had to invoke his special powers to promulgate the Bill as the Public Safety Ordinance. While the Government's seizure of their entire top leadership immensely weakened the Communists' striking power, the defiant resistance to the Government's action by the nationalists enabled people to see it as one more attack on civil liberties and constitutional propriety at the hands of imperialism.

The other target of the Government was the revolutionaries seeking to reorganize and revive their group. On 8 April Bhagat Singh and Batukeshwar Dutt threw bombs at the Central Assembly, to mark their protest, significantly enough, against the Public Safety Bill and the repressive Trade Disputes Bill. They wished to publicize their cause through their trial, which was short, both being sentenced to life transportation in June. Unfortunately, by now Bhagat Singh and his comrades were linked to Saunders' assassination. Practically the entire group was arrested, and their trial on this charge began in July. This, again, was a great blow; but the fact that the young men were sacrificing themselves for India not only made Bhagat Singh 'a symbol', but created a fresh source of bitterness against the British Government.[12] Their comrade Jatin Das's death on 13 September from a long fast over prison conditions spread grief all over the country, with over half a million people accompanying his coffin at Calcutta – Jawaharlal Nehru was to begin his presidential speech at the Lahore Congress on 29 December with a homage to Jatin Das and the Burmese martyr Vizaya.

Side by side with repression, the British Government attempted to entice away the moderate elements. It recognized that the Simon Commission was so far tarnished, and the several parties and groups so strongly committed to its boycott, that it was not practical politics to make any offers through its agency. On 31 October 1929 Irwin directly issued a declaration agreeing to a Round Table Conference of representatives of the British Government, and Indian parties and interests – which had been earlier a demand of the Congress itself. Secondly, in words characteristically hedged in with qualifications, it committed the British Government to a grant of 'Dominion Status', not now, but some time in future.[13]

The statement, so blatantly putting the Simon Commission in the limbo, won an initial response from the Congress and the Liberals; indeed, on 2 November, Gandhi, Motilal Nehru, Jawaharlal Nehru, Madan Mohan Malaviya, Tej Bahadur Sapru and others issued a joint statement at Delhi, welcoming the Irwin statement as indicative of the Government's 'desire ... to placate Indian opinion' and offering cooperation if certain substantive conditions (or 'points') were met. There may be reasons why Gandhi, though initially cautious, committed the Congress leadership to this ambiguous position: an expectation, perhaps, that under England's first Labour Government, that had recently taken office, India could hope for something better. Or, a hope that in return for an acceptance of the Irwin declaration, more specific constitutional and policy concessions might be obtained from the British Government. But the perilous walk into imperialism's parlour was blocked by two identifiable factors.

One was Subhas Bose's blunt refusal to endorse the Delhi statement followed by his resignation from the Congress Working Committee, and Jawaharlal's pangs of conscience and deep regret over it ('a bitter pill ... I allowed myself to be talked into signing').[14] But, perhaps, even more than the internal dissent in the nationalist camp, was the premature exposure of the real nature of the Irwin Declaration on the floors of the Houses of Parliament in London, in the very first week of November. The Labour Government's response to the ferocious Tory and Liberal onslaught on 'the Dominion status' concession was extremely tepid; and its spokesmen, including the Secretary of State for India, Wedgewood-Benn, argued that nothing new had been offered and that the Simon Commission's final authority remained unaffected. After this the Congress Working Committee, which had been compelled on 19 November to formally endorse the Delhi declaration, had no choice but to give it a quiet burial as well, by making its Delhi offer also subject to the year-end deadline.

In the end, it was only the Liberals and Responsivists, already left high and dry by the Congress's deadline for the All-parties' Report, who professed to remain delighted at the Irwin statement, and went off to London to attend the First Round Table Conference in 1930, when their co-signatories of the Delhi statement had been clapped into gaol. But if the Irwin statement was ephemeral, so was the following of these motley groups.

How a following could in fact be assembled was shown by Gandhi by the hectic campaign that 'beloved slave-driver' organized throughout 1929. He concentrated on the boycott of foreign cloth and promotion of khadi, and he toured various rural parts of the country carrying the message of his Constructive Programme. He devoted much attention to the mobilization of women and to the fight against untouchability. Of all the Congress leaders, he showed the most concern for furthering Hindu–Muslim understanding. While his negotiations with Jinnah (who had by now enlarged his earlier five proposals into '14 points') proved unsuccessful, Muslim leaders close to the Congress established (27 July) the Nationalist Muslim Party, avowedly to oppose communalism and take their 'proper share in the national struggle'. Its leaders included Abul Kalam Azad, Dr Ansari and Ch. Khaliquzzaman.

The efforts to expand the membership of the Congress, which now had Jawaharlal Nehru as one of its General Secretaries, were also important. Congress membership crossed the half a million mark by the end of the year (1929).[15] Despite inefficiency in reporting from some areas, it was clear that there was no other political organization in the country that could even remotely compare with the Congress in size and mobilizing power. For the critical annual session at Lahore, Gandhi's name was proposed for President in September; however, in an unexpected move, Gandhi not only refused the office for himself, but, sidelining the next name, Vallabhbhai Patel, insisted on Jawaharlal Nehru being elected as President. So Jawaharlal entered the office 'by a trap-door', elected by a 'bewildered' AICC, much to the President-elect's own discomfort.[16] Behind this decision was obviously Gandhi's sincere desire to build bridges with the radical ranks within the Congress, even if it weakened the dominance of his own philosophy over the movement.

Gandhi and Motilal Nehru, with Jinnah and Sapru as mediators, met Irwin on 23 December 1929. From both sides it turned out to be a formal statement of positions, Gandhi and Motilal insisting on the four conditions of the Delhi statement, and Irwin refusing to go beyond his own original declaration. There was, therefore, no doubt left that the deadline set by the Calcutta Congress would pass without any substantive concession made by the British Government.

IV

When the Lahore session of the Congress opened on 29 December 1929, the path was thus cleared for a direct call for a struggle to attain full independence – '*purna swaraj*' or '*azadi*', in the official terminology of the Congress. Jawaharlal Nehru's address was important for underlining this fact, and, no less too, for giving a vision of free India which was different both from that of the moderate constitutionalism of the earlier leadership and from Gandhi's nostalgia for a machineless village India, with the rich seen as trustees of the poor: Jawaharlal proudly proclaimed that he was 'a socialist and a republican'. Speaking of socialism, he asserted that 'India will have to go that way, too, if she seeks to end her poverty and inequality'.[17] This was to be a new basis for rallying the Indian poor to the cause of national freedom, and, from now on, this stress on equality and change in the property system was to find increasing assertion in Congress declarations.

There was an attempt, too, to assure Muslim and Sikh leaders of the readiness of the Congress to accommodate their claims. Jawaharlal said: 'So far as I am concerned I would gladly ask our Muslim and Sikh friends to take what they will without protest or argument from me.'[18] Gandhi reopened the issue of the communal 'solution' of the All-parties' Report, by saying that 'now that the Nehru Report on the lines of Dominion Status will be declared to have lapsed', he hoped that 'the Sikhs and Muslims and all other sections who had one or other grievances against the Nehru Report will see no objection' to uniting with the Congress in its struggle.[19] On this explicit basis the Congress passed a resolution 'assur[ing] the Sikhs, the Muslims and other minorities that no solution [of communal questions] ... in any future constitution will be acceptable to the Congress that does not give full satisfaction to the parties concerned'. It was, perhaps, entitled to hope that this assurance would clear up the misgivings entertained by Jinnah and others about the All-parties' Report. At the same time, the Congress spurned the British offer of a Round Table Conference and of conducting any negotiations under its aegis.

As immediate steps in the ensuing struggle, it was decided to call for resignations from the councils and a boycott of their elections, to organize a campaign to enrol Congress members and volunteers, and to hold public meetings. 26 January 1930 was to be observed as the Independence Day. On this day the national tricolour was unfurled at countless meetings throughout the country. Everywhere a pledge drafted by Gandhi was taken: it recited the major grievances of the Indian people against British rule, and declared that it would be 'a crime against man and God' to submit any longer to such rule. The British Government also began its own onslaught: just three days before the Independence Day, Subhas Bose was sentenced to a year's rigorous imprisonment on charges of sedition and conspiracy.

The campaign of civil disobedience was yet to begin; in effect, its date and form had been left to Gandhi to determine. He had, as late as September 1929, denied that 'the masses are impatient to be led to civil disobedience',[20] and he was now clearly anxious about creating intermediate slogans for mobilization. His 'eleven points' in *Young India*,[21] ostensibly in reply to a speech by Irwin, were clearly addressed not so much to the British Government as to the various sections of the Indian people. The peasants were to be enticed by the demand for a 50 per cent reduction in land revenue, to be made possible by corresponding reductions in military expenditure and salaries in 'higher grade services'; and all the poor, generally, would benefit from the abolition of the salt tax. 'Protective tariff on foreign cloth' would appeal to the millions of hand-spinners and weavers, as well as the industrialists and workers in the modern textile industry; the demand for the devaluation of the rupee to 1s.4d. and the reservation of coastal traffic to Indian shipping were designed to harness the sympathies of Indian capital. Total prohibition had religious appeal for both Hindus and Muslims, and Gandhi had been appealing to women particularly to support it. Finally, the discharge of political prisoners, abolition of the C.I.D. and issue of fire-arm licenses represented preliminary political demands affecting both the nationalists and ordinary people.[22]

One can imagine Gandhi subsequently scanning this list and narrowing the choice of the target for the initial offensive to point no. 4, 'abolition of the salt tax'. This was an entirely regressive tax: its collection in 1929–30 amounted to Rs 6.76 crores, a sum equal to two-fifths of the realization from income tax. The salt duty not only fell heavily upon the poor, but its levy necessitated bans on small, local salt-makers. In line with Gandhi's strategic thought, the demand for its abolition was moderate and reasonable (after all, salt duty did not exceed 8.5 per cent of the total central revenues), while, by doubling the price of salt in most areas, it affected a very large number of people. Moreover, it was a cause with which the poor would identify. After obtaining an explicit authorization from the Congress Working Committee (14–16 February), Gandhi announced the decision to begin the satyagraha in a letter of 2 March to Irwin; and on 12 March 1930 he began it by starting on the famous Dandi March from his Sabarmati Ashram at Ahmedabad to Dandi on the Gujarat coast, where salt could be made from pans. As the 241-mile-long march proceeded, the numbers of the satyagrahis grew as well as of those who attended his meetings, in which, incidentally, he insisted on participation by the 'untouchables' as equals. The degree of local support was shown by the fact that, according to official reports, 227 village headmen in the area resigned their posts as part of non-cooperation. On 6 April Gandhi and his companions defiantly broke the law by extracting salt. The news caused great excitement and similar salt-making satyagrahas were organized all over the country. On 14 April Jawaharlal Nehru was arrested, to be tried and sentenced to six months' imprisonment under the Salt Act. Vitthalbhai Patel, President of the Central Assembly (not now technically a Congress member), resigned from the Assembly, as did Malaviya (who had opposed Civil Disobedience), on 25 April.

The growing nationalist upsurge inspired Surjya Sen and his fellow revolutionaries of 'the Indian Republican Army' to carry out a very bold undertaking, the Chittagong armoury raid on 18 April. Having seized the police and auxiliary force armouries that night, they retreated to the hills, where, on 22 April, they fought a battle with British troops, with fatalities on both sides. Thereafter they dispersed, Surjya Sen himself eluding capture for nearly three years, but dying a martyr's death on 12 January 1934.

As repression grew (the Press Ordinance to muzzle the press was imposed on 27 April), the popular resistance also grew; and in late April Peshawar, on the other side of Chittagong, seemed to become for the moment the storm-centre of the movement.

Khan Abdul Ghaffar Khan, the legendary Pathan leader, had attended both the Calcutta and Lahore sessions of the Congress, and had made active preparations for Civil Disobedience, the membership of his volunteer Pakhtoon organization, 'Khudai Khidmatgars' (popularly known as 'Red Shirts'), reaching an estimated 50,000. On 19 April, Abdul Ghaffar Khan began Civil Disobedience with a mass meeting at his village of Utmanzai; and the picketing of liquor shops was set to begin at Peshawar from 23 April. Early on that day, however, the Government acted, and Abdul Ghaffar Khan and the other main leaders were arrested. As a protesting crowd gathered at the Kabuli Gate at Peshawar, British troops were brought in with armoured cars. When the indignant crowd did not disperse, they opened fire from machine-guns, which continued for hours, until by the evening about 200 to 250 lay dead (official 'count': 30). Martial law was then imposed. It was all so reminiscent of Jallianwala Bagh – in all but one respect, however: troops of the Royal Garhwal Rifles disobeyed orders and refused to open fire. They continued their stoic defiance even when the crowd, maddened by the firing from British troops, threw brickbats and missiles, injuring the Garhwalis. Removed from the scene and then to their barracks, the Garhwalis refused to return to the city; they simply said, they could not open fire on their countrymen. Guarded by British troops (for the Sikh Regiment refused the duty), they surrendered their arms; 67 of them were subjected to court martial and received heavy sentences, including life imprisonment. However, no court martial in the world could deny to these Garhwalis the place they came to occupy in the hearts of the Indian people.

Peshawar itself remained unsubdued until 4 May, when British control was reasserted over the city. The same night (4/5 May) Gandhi was arrested under a Regulation of 1827 that made it possible to detain him without trial. Lord Irwin, who in April had been hopefully speaking of an astrological prediction of Gandhi's death, had now to face the situation he had so much feared: India's reaction to Gandhi's incarceration.

The wave of protest first struck Bombay, the news sending people into the streets in such large numbers as to cause a general withdrawal of the police. Textile workers and railwaymen were out in thousands; cloth merchants were on a six-day hartal. Police resorted to firing at protesting crowds in Calcutta and Delhi. Troops had to be used in Peshawar again and in Kohat in mid-May. But it was the industrial town of Sholapur which now repeated the April exploits of Peshawar. On 7 May, as the textile workers came out on strike, British authority was violently overthrown (some policemen being killed), liquor shops were set on fire and control by Congress volunteers was established over the town. The government's writ could be re-established only after the imposition of martial law on 16 May.

Before his arrest Gandhi was planning a new satyagraha at the Dharasana salt-works in Gujarat. Now, Sarojini Naidu and Imam Saheb (Gandhi's colleague of South Africans days) led some 2,500 marchers on 21 May. 'Suddenly,' reported an eye-witness, the American journalist Webb Miller,

> at a word of command, scores of native policemen rushed upon the advancing marchers and rained blows on their head with their steel-shod lathis. Not one of the marchers even raised an arm to fend off the blows. ... Those struck down fell sprawling unconscious of writhing with fractured skulls or broken shoulders. The survivors, without breaking ranks, silently and doggedly marched on until struck down.[23]

Nothing better brings out the bias of 'the Cambridge school' with its silent supposition that Englishmen could never lie, while the word of Indians is always suspect, than Judith Brown's attribution of the 'blood-curdling accounts of police brutality' to the 'excellent publicity machine of the Congress': the 'savage police beatings' did not, of course, occur, for were they not 'refuted' by the Government – some three weeks after the incident, on 11 June?[24]

The Salt Satyagraha in the meantime grew almost spontaneously into a mass satyagraha. Everywhere merchants and shopkeepers dealing in foreign cloth (especially English) had to face picketing and social boycott; the unpopular forest laws were defied in Maharashtra, Karnataka and Central Provinces. A new phase began when peasants in Gujarat, starting from Bardoli (10 May), refused to pay revenue, braving the seizure of their crops and lands. In Midnapore district of

Bengal, peasant defiance took the form of refusal to pay *chowkidar* tax.

The Government replied by the Prevention of Intimidation Ordinance and the Unlawful Instigation Ordinance, both promulgated on 30 May. On 20 July came the News-sheets and Newspapers Ordinance, followed on 10 October by the Unlawful Association Ordinance. Correspondence came under censorship, the Congress and its associate organizations were declared illegal, and their funds made subject to seizure.

These measures did not appear to have any effect on the movement. Even Muslim nationalists, like Dr M.A. Ansari, who had been critical of the Lahore decision to launch Civil Disobedience, trained their guns on the British Government; Syed Mahmud, Tasadduq Sherwani and Rafi Kidwai now went to jail. So did Madan Mohan Malaviya. The overall strong middle-class support to the movement was shown in the elections in September 1930, where the Congress-imposed boycott in the limited electorates forced a fall from a poll percentage of 48.07 in the previous elections (1926) to a mere 26.1 in the elections held now for the central legislative assembly; in the provincial councils a similar trend was noticeable in all provinces, but the sharpest fall was in Bombay, from 48.2 in 1926 to 16.5 in 1930. The decline also extended to most Muslim constituencies in the provincial council elections, but it was significantly less sharp than in the general (non-Muslim) constituencies.[25] The large numbers of persons courting arrest exceeded all expectations. Official reports (bound to be conservative) indicated that 29,054 persons were in prison in connection with Civil Disobedience in mid-November 1930. Of these, 359 were women and 1,150 Muslims. While the spread of the movement had local variations, pockets of intense activity existing side by side with relatively quiet areas – an unevenness on which much stress has been laid in recent work – a large degree of participation was seen in towns, and the movement was undoubtedly making significant gains in the villages.

The Civil Disobedience Movement coincided with the onset of the most critical period of the 1929–32 Depression. The weighted index of agricultural prices shows that prices had been declining since 1926 (when it was 283), but in 1930 there was a sudden dip, from 252 (in 1929) to 206. Such a fall meant that peasants would find it very hard to pay the zamindars (landlords) the cash rents due to the latter, or to repay their loans to the usurers, or, in areas where they were the revenue payers themselves, to pay the revenue to government. In Gujarat, where the last situation prevailed, the battle had been entered in right earnest in May itself. And now the conflagration spread as the peasants, in increasing numbers, saw their financial salvation in Civil Disobedience. At the same time, the Depression affected the towns differently. The rising unemployment (together with the organizational effects of the Meerut case imprisonments) greatly reduced working-class militancy (reflected in a mere 2.2 million working days lost in 1930, compared with 12.2 million in 1929). Urban middle-class participation had perhaps also passed its zenith by the autumn.

When Jawaharlal Nehru came out of prison (briefly, as it turned out) on 11 October 1930, he immediately saw the duality in the situation: there was a vast opportunity offered for a no-tax campaign among peasants, but where peasants were zamindars' tenants, as in U.P., this could only become a no-rent campaign and, therefore, raise a 'class issue'. On the other hand, the existing Civil Disobedience campaign was 'getting a bit stale'; and 'the cities and middle classes were a bit tired of hartals and processions'. Nehru's instinctive answer to this dilemma was to take the bull by the horns. If a 'fresh infusion of blood' had to come, it had to be from the peasantry – 'the reserve stocks there were enormous'. Civil Disobedience would, then, 'again become a mass movement, touching the vital interests of the masses'.[26] About 1,600 delegates gathered at Allahabad on 19 October, to open 'a no-tax campaign' in the district. Jawaharlal spoke at the gathering and was promptly re-arrested, and sentenced to a total of two years' rigorous imprisonment with a further five months in default of fines.

The sentence on Jawaharlal Nehru was illustrative of the kind of treatment the civil resisters were getting. Floggings began to occur in prisons. According to an official estimate, there were still in February 1931 some 23–24,000 Civil Disobedience prisoners, and the total number of those who had been through jail was put at 60,000. The AICC reported 92,000 convictions during the period up to the suspension of the movement in March 1931. The massive impact of the movement was seen in the dramatic fall in the consumption of British cloth, the import of British cotton piece-goods falling precipitately from 1,248 million yards in 1929–30 to only 543 million yards in 1930–31; and this despite a great fall in prices in the ratio of 26.0 to 22.5 per unit of all foreign cloth imported. The psychological shift among the Indian consumers was so profound that the share in the Indian market now lost by Britain was never regained.[27]

V

On 26 January 1931, on the very first anniversary of the Independence pledge, all members of the Congress Working Committee were released, including Gandhi and Jawaharlal Nehru. The unconditional release signalled the British Government's wish to have another attempt at negotiations.

An earlier abortive attempt had been made through mediators in August 1930. Motilal Nehru and Jawaharlal Nehru had been taken form Naini Jail to Yeravada Jail to meet Gandhi, in order to frame the Congress response to the British Government's desire that the Congress take part in the First Round Table Conference. The Congress leaders countered with a strong demand for some prior British commitment to India's right to secede from the empire. The first Round Table Conference was, therefore, a meeting between British politicians in London (12 November 1930 to 19 January 1931) with motley loyalist, 'liberal' and communal leaders, and Princes' representatives, which resulted in nothing substantial – partly because these groups could not agree among themselves on any point, and partly because without their commanding any influence over any section of Indian opinion, their agreement was politically worthless. On the closing day of the Conference the British Prime Minister, Ramsay MacDonald, made a speech which seemed to lay before India the very limited perspective of the grant of 'responsible' government in the provinces; a 'federation', which would include the Princes with their internal powers unimpaired; and the continuance of British authority over the army, external relations and the protection of British economic interests and of minorities. The Conference was to be convened again. On 17 January Lord Irwin, in his speech to the Central Assembly, uttering sweet words about Gandhi ('no one can fail to recognize the spiritual force which impels Mr Gandhi to count no sacrifice too great in the cause, as he believes, of the India he loves'), invited him and the Congress to participate in the Second Round Table Conference.

It is more or less clear why the British Government should have endeavoured once again to achieve an end to the Civil Disobedience by conceding nothing substantial. What was being offered, only in the form of vague principles, was severely constrained: 'self-government' was a far cry from dominion status, let alone '*purna swaraj*'. All methods of repression had failed to bring the Civil Disobedience Movement to heel; and already in December 1930, Irwin had admitted to the Secretary of the State that the administration had 'been subject to continuous strain for nearly nine months', and 'we cannot afford to allow the strain to get heavier'.[28] There was some official alarm by March at the Congress organizing a movement against full-rent payment in U.P.; and even a friend of the British Government, Tej Bahadur Sapru, admitted (25 March) that the economic situation of the U.P. peasants was 'very bad', and that 'they have been thoroughly infected by the "no-rent" doctrines'.[29] If victory could not be forced over the Congress in these conditions, a truce could be of inestimable advantage to the Government.

What does not come out immediately so clearly is why the Congress leadership and Gandhi, in particular, should reverse the position taken at Yeravada in August and move towards a truce. Sumit Sarkar has argued that Indian big business pressure was now at work. Indian industrial houses had been placated by a surcharge of 5 per cent on imported piece-goods imposed in February 1931; and he quotes D.P. Khaitan's speech as President of the Indian Chamber of Commerce, 11 February, suggesting 'to Mahatma Gandhi and the Congress that the time has come when they should explore the possibilities of an honourable settlement. ... We all want peace.' Sir Purushottamdas Thakurdas, the leading industrialist of Bombay, had invited the ire of the Congress in November 1930 by giving a farewell dinner to the Bombay police commissioner; now, he was the principal business representative trying to persuade Gandhi to go to the negotiating table.[30] Gandhi could not wholly ignore the opinion of this class, however much his own backers from amongst its ranks (like Ambalal Sarabhai and G.D. Birla) remained loyal and appeared unassertive.

It is yet possible that the principal factor motivating a compromise lay elsewhere: in an appreciation that the satyagraha as conducted till hitherto was losing steam; and neither Gandhi nor the Congress were either ideologically or organizationally prepared to harness the vast reserves of peasant unrest over rent that Nehru had spoken of. There was, first, the tactical disadvantage that 'neither government nor the big zamindars took any widespread action to terrorize the recalcitrant tenantry for several months',[31] so that a political confrontation could not immediately emerge. Secondly, the Congress organization itself had a large number of zamindars and was hardly in a shape to lead an anti-zamindar agitation. Moreover, Nehru himself acknowledges that there was little presence of an agrarian orientation in the Congress in provinces other than U.P.[32]

The danger in letting the Civil Disobedience Movement lose its momentum without a compromise was that demoralization would thereupon set in among those who had been imprisoned, and whose property and official posts had been forfeited. Their situation weighed heavily on Gandhi's mind as he and the Congress Working Committee proceeded to take the fateful decision for negotiations that they did. Motilal Nehru's death (6 February 1931) had deprived the top Congress leadership of an old moderate who, in his last days, had taken a very uncompromising stand; and his absence tended to isolate Jawaharlal in his forlorn struggle against the current.

The surrounding circumstances were still by no means propitious for a compromise. Chandrashekhar Azad, the well-known revolutionary, died in an encounter with the police at Allahabad on 27 February 1931. On 7 October 1930, Bhagat Singh, Sukhdev and Rajguru had been sentenced to death by the special tribunal, and their hanging was set for 23 March 1931. All India was anxious for the saving of their young lives; but it was clear that the British Government would exclude the case from its negotiations with the Congress.

Conversations took place between Gandhi and Irwin at the Viceregal Lodge, Delhi, beginning on 27 February; and on 5 March the official *Gazette of India Extraordinary* published the terms of the Gandhi–Irwin agreement.[33] By it, the Civil Disobedience Movement of the Congress was to be 'discontinued' (not withdrawn), while the Government would release all political prisoners and withdraw the

Ordinances issued during the period of Civil Disobedience as well as the notifications of unlawful associations. The agreement went into detail in defining what the Congress could not do (e.g., undertake defiance of laws, agitate for 'non-payment of revenue', resort to aggressive picketing); on the other hand, the matter of inquiries against the police was explicitly shelved. Government grant of release would not apply to prisoners convicted of or charged with violence. Civil resisters' land and immovable property that had been confiscated would be returned, but not if it had been 'sold to third parties'. Posts from which supporters of the movement had been removed might be restored to them if no fresh permanent appointments had been made. The ban on salt-making would be lifted for those who did not make it for the general market. As for the larger political settlement, the principles of Ramsay MacDonald's speech of 19 January were to be made the basis for 'the participation of the representatives of the Congress in the further discussions ... on the scheme of constitutional reform'.

The announcement of the Gandhi–Irwin pact was greeted by the Congress rank and file as a great success. Within a few days, some 14,000 of the political prisoners were released;[34] and as they came out, they received warm public receptions in their towns and villages. It appeared to them, as it did to Winston Churchill, the inveterate enemy of Indian freedom, that the British Viceroy had at last been forced into negotiating with Gandhi 'as an equal and as if he [Gandhi] were the victor in some warlike encounter' (Churchill's speech, 12 March). It could be argued that the truce would give time to the Congress to consolidate and reopen the struggle even more vigorously, if the promised 'constitutional reform' proved to be inadequate. Indeed, the Government seemed much troubled by these countrywide celebrations of triumph which seemed to give to the Congress so much added prestige and strength.[35]

But those who had thought of an uncompromising struggle for independence, like Jawaharlal Nehru and Subhas Bose, were left to wonder if all the sound and fury had not ended in 'a whimper'.[36] Their premonitions proved to be justified. Even the promises of the MacDonald statement were not fulfilled. It took more than four years for the British Parliament to embody them, under the most restrictive interpretation, in the Government of India Act, 1935; and two years more had to pass before this Act's provisions for 'Provincial Autonomy' were implemented (after the 1937 elections). The provisions for sharing 'responsibility' at the centre were never put into effect, the Government of India Act, 1919, remaining in force in part right up to 1947. The absence of a time-frame deprived all constitutional pledges of any meaning. There were others outside the Congress too who protested. On 16 March, at a labour meeting at Parel, Bombay, Gandhi confronted Communist hecklers who taunted him for forgetting the Meerut accused, his own eleven points and 'the substance of Independence'.[37] But the most emotional outcry came from the supporters of the revolutionaries who felt that enough had not been done for saving Bhagat Singh, who, with his two comrades, went to the gallows on 23 March, head high to the last.

The Gandhi–Irwin pact was to be presented to the Congress meeting at Karachi, due in the last week of March 1931. Despite some public demonstrations against Gandhi by groups of radical youth, the Congress passed (29 March) a resolution approving the terms of 'the provisional settlement', but asserting that the Congress goal of *purna swaraj* (complete independence) 'remains intact'.[38] What was potentially far more important, however, was a resolution on 'fundamental rights and economic changes'. The text was originally drafted by Jawaharlal Nehru, and revised by Gandhi. Though the extent of revision it underwent from Gandhiji's hands is not known, the result contained substantial departures from the Gandhian creed. The resolution demanded 'substantial reduction in agricultural rent or revenue paid by the peasantry, and in case of uneconomic holdings exemption from rent'. In his speech on the resolution Gandhi made it clear that legislation, not persuasion, would be the instrument to bring it into effect, though he appealed to the zamindars to anticipate the coming legislation. Similarly, the point about 'control of usury' meant, in Gandhi's own exposition of it, that legislation for 'drastic reductions' in rates of interest would be on the agenda. Five out of the twenty points related to protection and rights of the working class. Finally, 'control by the State of key industries and ownership of mineral resources' was a remarkable concession to the socialist aspirations growing within the Congress ranks. There were also assurances of the abolition of caste disabilities, equal rights for women and protection to minorities (with the state obliged to maintain 'religious neutrality'), on which, of course, there had hardly been any differences hitherto between Gandhi and the radicals.[39]

The short resolution was expanded later by the AICC into a full-fledged programme, offering what is essentially the vision of a modern, secular democracy with welfare policies and planned industrial development under state aegis. The Congress now had a social and economic platform with which it hoped it could rally peasants, workers, women and minorities.

The Karachi Resolution as a blue-print of free India was an important achievement: to Sir Tej Bahadur Sapru, it appeared a tactical move to win endorsement of the Gandhi–Irwin agreement, but still 'a heavy price for the allegiance of Jawaharlal'.[40] But there is no doubt that Gandhi had himself come round to the view that the 'reserves' of the peasants and workers could not be called up for the battle for freedom without some promises of change in the land system and the industrial order. It was on an appeal to these promises that the national movement henceforth heavily relied for mass mobilization.[41]

New days of trial would come soon: Congress leaders and functionaries in thousands were put in prison again in 1932 when Civil Disobedience was renewed, with convictions approaching 75,000 by April 1933. In 1940 imprisonments began again; and with Quit India (1942), prison entry had yet another cycle. All through these hard times the Indian people remained unswerving in their loyalty to the national movement; and the Karachi programme reaffirmed again and again by the Congress remained a beacon-light for them. Whenever we celebrate our freedom, the Karachi Resolution must surely be the touchstone by which we can test how far the promises made to those who worked and suffered for our freedom have been fulfilled.

Notes

[1] This was through the insertion of Section 84A into the Government of India Act, 1915. The words 'to restrict' are also included in the text of the Royal appointment of the Simon Commission, formally issued on 26 November 1927.

[2] A significant pointer to the incorporation of a part of the British Labour Party in this establishment was the inclusion of two Labour members; one of whom was the future Labour Prime Minister, Clement Attlee.

[3] P. Das Gupta's revised estimates on census age distribution, *Population Studies*, XXV (1971), tabulated by L. and P. Visaria in *Cambridge Economic History of India*, Vol. II, Cambridge, 1983, p. 502.

[4] J. Coatman, *India in 1927–28*, Official Government of India Statement laid before Parliament, Calcutta, 1928, p. 61.

[5] Quoted in Stanley Wolpert, *Jinnah of Pakistan*, New York, 1984, p. 90.

[6] Quoted, ibid., p. 93.

[7] *An Autobiography*, London, 1936, pp. 184–85, but see p. 172.

[8] *Documents of the History of the Communist Party of India*, edited by G. Adhikari, Vol. III C (1928), New Delhi, 1982, p. 218.

[9] Tara Chand, *History of the Freedom Movement*, Publication Division, Government of India, New Delhi, 1972, Vol. IV, pp. 111–16.

[10] For example, Paragraph 23(c) of the Recommendations implied that there could be Departments not administered by members of the Executive Council responsible to the Legislature.

[11] Text as summarized by Judith M. Brown, *Gandhi and Civil Disobedience*, Cambridge, 1977, p. 60.

[12] 'He become a symbol; the act [Saunders' assassination] was forgotten, the symbol remained, and within a few months [of his arrest] each town and village of the Punjab, and to a lesser extent in the rest of northern India, resounded with his name' (Nehru, *Autobiography*, p. 175).

[13] 'I am authorized, on behalf of His Majesty's Government, to state clearly that, in their judgement, it is implicit in the [Montagu] Declaration of 1917 that the natural issue of India's constitutional progress, as there contemplated, is the attainment of Dominion Status.' The 1917 Declaration had contemplated a stage-by-stage 'gradual development of self-governing institutions'.

[14] *Autobiography*, p. 197.

[15] The total being 5,10,276 as reported to the AICC before the Lahore session of the Congress (Brown, *Gandhi and Civil Disobedience*, p. 52).

[16] J. Nehru, *An Autobiography*, pp. 194–95.

[17] *Selected Works of Jawaharlal Nehru*, edited by S. Gopal, Vol. IV, Delhi, 1973, p. 192.

[18] Ibid., p. 187.

[19] Gandhi at Subjects Committee, AICC, 27 December 1929: *Collected Works of Mahatma Gandhi*, Vol. XLII, New Delhi, 1970, p. 324.

[20] *Collected Works*, Vol. XLI, p. 519.

[21] *Collected Works*, Vol. XLII, pp. 432–35.

[22] Nehru saw these points as 'a surprising development', a come-down from 'independence' (*Autobiography*, p. 210); for much harsher criticism on this score, see R.P. Dutt, *India Today*, Bombay, 1947, p. 298. Judith Brown's analysis seems to me more reasonable here (*Gandhi and Civil Disobedience*, pp. 922–23).

[23] Quoted from Fischer, *The Life of Mahama Gandhi*, in Tara Chand, Vol. IV, p. 127.

[24] Brown, *Gandhi and Civil Disobedience*, pp. 113–14. Brown does not pause to

think how the Congress 'publicity machine' could have worked, when its pamphlet, *The Black Regime at Dharasana*, was promptly banned and its copies confiscated.

[25] See the useful tables in Brown, pp. 390–93.

[26] *Autobiography*, pp. 131–32.

[27] See the table, 'Gross Imports of Cotton Piece-goods into India, 1900–1 to 1939–40', in Amiya Kumar Bagchi, *Private Investment in India, 1900–1939*, Cambridge, 1972, p. 238.

[28] Telegram, 20 December, quoted by Brown, pp. 168–69.

[29] Quoted, ibid., p. 198.

[30] Sumit Sarkar, 'The Logic of Gandhian Nationalism', *Indian Historical Review*, III (1), 1976, esp., pp. 136–41.

[31] *Autobiography*, p. 237. But Gandhi in his conversations with the Home Secretary H.W. Emerson on 6 April 1931 did refer to 'brutal treatment of tenants by landlords' in U.P. (*Collected Works of Mahatma Gandhi*, Vol. XLV, p. 454). It is interesting that Emerson was all the time trying to impart to the tenant–landlord struggle a communal colouring, by stressing the exceptional cases of Hindu tenants vs. Muslim landlords.

[32] *Autobiography*, p. 238.

[33] The text is conveniently given in *Collected Works of Mahatma Gandhi*, Vol. XLV, pp. 432–36.

[34] *Collected Works of Mahatma Gandhi*, Vol. XLV, p. 324: Irwin's report of his statement made to Gandhi on 19 March. The cases of the remaining political prisoners were 'being examined'.

[35] J. Nehru, *Autobiography*, p. 263.

[36] Ibid., p. 259.

[37] For Gandhi's own conciliatory, though rather patronizing reply, see *Collected Works*, Vol. LXV, pp. 298–300.

[38] Ibid., p. 363.

[39] See both for the original resolution and Gandhi's speech, ibid., pp.370–74.

[40] Quoted in Brown, p. 203.

[41] The Karachi Resolution was reaffirmed, for example, in the Congress election manifesto of December 1936.

5

The Left and the National Movement

Marx and Indian Liberation

What has come to be defined as the 'Left' in the historiography of the National Movement and current political discourse is essentially the assemblage of all elements as owed allegiance to the socialist world-outlook. It is an area in which Marxism exercised the dominant influence. While it is true that, as a standard-bearer of the working class in the struggle against capitalism, Marx's main theoretical writings were concerned with the 'laws of motion' of capitalism and the capitalist exploitation of labour, it is important to remember that his commitment to the cause of India's national liberation pre-dated any recognizable beginnings of our own National Movement. In 1853 he wrote in an American newspaper, the *New York Daily Tribune:*

> The Indians will not reap the fruits of the new elements of society scattered among them by the British bourgeoisie, till in Great Britain itself the new ruling classes shall have been supplanted by the industrial proletariat, or *till the Hindus [Indians] themselves shall have grown strong enough to throw off the English yoke altogether.* (Our italics)

When the Great Revolt of 1857 broke out, Marx and Engels were consistent in their defence of the rebels and in condemnation of British atrocities in their writings in the same newspaper.[1] This needs to be particularly stressed because some radical writers such as Edward Said

This text was prepared for the P. Sundarayya Memorial Lecture, Hyderabad, May 1998. Like the preceding essay, it was also included in SAHMAT's volume, *Indian People in the Struggle for Freedom,* New Delhi, 1998.

have been taking Marx to task for an alleged lack of sympathy for the Indian people.[2]

There is no evidence of any direct personal contact between Marx and any Indian opponent of British rule. In 1871, the General Council of the International Workingmen's Association, in which Marx was the moving spirit, received a letter from an unidentified supporter from Calcutta, drawing attention to the 'great discontent ... among the people' and 'the wretched conditions of the workers' in India; little is known about the sequel, though the General Council advised the correspondent to open a branch of the International with special attention to 'enrolling natives'.[3] An indirect contact with Dadabhai Naoroji, India's indefatigable spokesman in London, could have developed through H.M. Hyndman, one of England's early social democrats. He maintained good relations with Marx until the summer of 1881, and was also a friend of Dadabhai Naoroji, who describes him as a 'friend of India'.[4]

Some statements by Marx in a letter of early 1881 echo Naoroji's calculations of the enormous burden of the tribute on India as well as his suggestion of the existence of popular conspiracies against the British, feeding on mass unrest.[5] Unfortunately, Hyndman's break with Marx later that year precluded the possibility of any personal association of Marx with Naoroji.

World Socialist Movement and National Liberation

Karl Marx died in 1883. Within a few years of his death two important developments took place, giving organizational forms to both Indian nationalism and international socialism. The Indian National Congress was founded in 1885 at Bombay; and the Second International in 1889 at Paris, the latter uniting under its banner the most advanced sections of the working-class movement of Europe and America. Unfortunately, owing to the very moderate constitutionalist politics of the Congress and the growing dominance of right-wing Social Democracy in the Second International, the two movements remained distant from each other. Dadabhai Naoroji, who had presided over the Congress at Calcutta in 1886 (and was to do so again in 1906), appeared at the Amsterdam Congress of the International in 1904, proclaiming the confidence of the Indian nationalists in the support of the

British working class; and Madame Cama, friend of revolutionary exiles, unfurled the tricolour (red, white and green) of Free India at the Stuttgart Congress of the International (1907). But these were, by and large, just episodes. Indeed, at Stuttgart itself an alliance of the left and centre only barely managed to delete from the resolution on the colonial problem a reference to the current civilizing colonial mission that would be taken over by the metropolitan socialist regimes after capitalism had been overthrown![6]

It was the revolutionary Marxists within the Second International who began to build a vision in which the proletariat's struggle for socialism would have an indispensable ally in the colonial peoples struggling for their national liberation. Lenin gave expression to this understanding in his article 'Inflammable Material in World Politics' (1908).[7] Surveying recent events in Iran, Turkey, India and China, he identified Japan as a model (and, therefore, a non-socialist or bourgeois–nationalist model) towards which the nations of the East were feeling themselves drawn.[8] Yet this did not prevent him from enthusiastically greeting the colonial people as allies against the common enemy, capitalist imperialism. His remarks on India were particularly important, with their reference to the demonstrations and strike in Bombay in protest against the sentencing of 'the democrat' Tilak to six years' imprisonment. The event drew from him the confident assertion that 'class-conscious workers of Europe now have Asiatic comrades and their number will grow by leaps and bounds'.[9]

Soviet Revolution and the Communist International

But until the Soviet revolution of 1917 there did not yet exist a socialist component within the national liberation movement. Even in 1914, Lenin was speaking of 'the possible correlations between the bourgeois liberation movements of the oppressed nations and the proletarian emancipation movement of the oppressing nation',[10] as if the former process had to be necessarily bourgeois in character. But 'the salvoes of the October Revolution' broke the separation; they did not only bring Marxism–Leninism to China, as Mao Zedong acknowledged,[11] but began to spread socialist ideas in all the major enslaved countries of the world. Once this happened, the socialist movement would no longer be an outside sympathetic spectator of the national

movement, but a distinct part of it; and its relationship with the hitherto dominant 'bourgeois–democratic' component consequentially
became a crucial question of Left revolutionary strategy on the world
scale.

At the Second Congress of the newly founded Communist International (Comintern) in July 1920, Lenin dealt with the new perspective both in his Preliminary Theses on the National–Colonial Question, and in his speech presenting the Theses.[12] He acknowledged that
in the circumstances of the time 'every nationalist movement [in the
colonial countries] can only be a bourgeois democratic movement,
for the bulk of the population in backward countries are peasants who
represent bourgeois–capitalist relations'. But the reality also was that
'very often, even in the majority of cases, perhaps, where the bourgeoisie of the oppressed countries does support the national movement, it
simultaneously works in harmony with the imperialist bourgeoisie,
i.e., it joins the latter in fighting against all revolutionary movements
and revolutionary classes'. Thus within the bourgeois–democratic
movements 'the revolutionary' elements were to be distinguished from
the 'reformist'. Communists were 'to support bourgeois liberation
movements in the colonial countries when these are really revolutionary'. But the term 'revolutionary' was given a surprisingly moderate meaning: it would apply wherever the bourgeois nationalists 'do
not hinder us in training and organizing the peasants and broad masses
of the exploited in a revolutionary spirit'. This complemented the call
to 'form independent cadres of [Communist] fighters, of Party organizations in all colonies and backward countries', who would come forward to organize the masses. But what vision of the future were the
Communists to present to the oppressed people? Could they project
the inevitability of capitalistic development, of which Lenin himself
had spoken earlier in his speech? On the contrary: they were required
by him to strive for the backward countries' passing, through a form of
'the Soviet system', 'to Communism', without undergoing the capitalist stage of development.[13] In other words, while supporting revolutionary bourgeois nationalists in a kind of alliance of mutual tolerance, the Communists would still project a rival blue-print for the
nation after its liberation.

This was, in fact, what Stalin was to say specifically for India in

1925, calling upon the Communist Party to 'enter into an open bloc with the revolutionary wing of the bourgeoisie in order, after isolating the compromising [section of the] national bourgeoisie, to lead the vast masses of the urban and rural petty-bourgeoisie in the struggle against imperialism'.[14]

The call for the formation of Communist organizations in colonial countries encouraged M.N. Roy to travel to Tashkent, where a number of Muslim exiles *(muhajirin)* from India had gathered. Upon some of the *muhajirs* being persuaded to come over to communism, a Communist Party of India was formed in October 1920 at Tashkent. Its headquarters moved with Roy, who constantly made an effort to send Communists trained abroad to India. Here, unluckily, they were rapidly tracked down, and received barbarously heavy sentences, notably in what came to be known as the Peshawar Conspiracy Cases (1921–23).

These early efforts, however abortive, have their place in the formation of a Left movement in India, and the names of the early Communist freedom-fighters (Muhammad Akbar Khan, sentenced to seven years' rigorous imprisonment, and others similarly sentenced but to shorter periods) need to be gratefully remembered. But the real impetus for the emergence of the Left came from within the country.

Emergence of Socialist and Left Ideas in India

On the issue of Indian independence as well as solidarity with Turkish resistance during the Khilafat Movement (1920–22), Indian nationalism and Soviet Russia were on the same side. This fact alone could not but have spread sympathy for the Soviet cause in large sections of nationalist opinion. But there was one more profound reason which provided a fertile ground for socialist ideas in India, viz. the nationalists' concern with India's poverty.

In their critique of British rule, the founding fathers of the Indian National Congress had made the Indi   eople's poverty a central issue. Dadabhai Naoroji, from 1876, wrote papers, memoranda and pamphlets statistically presenting the state of misery and tracing its causes to the tribute rendered to Britain, to the deindustrialization generated by Free Trade, and to over-taxation and currency manipulations by the British regime. Naoroji's writings were assembled and published in 1901 through Swan Sonnenchein & Co., London, who

were incidentally also the publishers of the Engels-edited English translation of Marx's *Capital*, London, 1887. In 1901 Romesh Dutt also
published his *Economic History of India under Early British Rule*, followed two years later (1903) by its companion volume, *The Economic
History of India in the Victorian Age*, the whole work constituting a
narration of the processes of Britain's exploitation of India. How massive the nationalist literature was on India's impoverishment by the
beginning of the twentieth century can be judged from Bipan Chandra's
very comprehensive study of it.[15] Simplified versions of the nationalist
perceptions of British exploitation were widely circulated: one good
example is offered by Gandhi's *Hind Suaraj*, written in 1909. It is true
that the nationalists trained their guns mainly on British rulers, and
were largely silent on the travails of labour in the Indian-owned fac-
tories and on peasants oppressed by the increasing rent extraction by
land-owners. Yet, once poverty of the masses was made a criterion for
identifying the oppressor, it was inevitable that the Indian capitalists
and land-owners could soon be so identified. The early peasant mobilization initiated by Gandhiji in 1917–18, in Champaran and Kheda,
were carefully selective in that the Indian land-owners were not involved. But the Ahmedabad textile workers' agitation of 1918 brought
Gandhi in confrontation with his own supporters, the cotton mill-
owners. Clearly, the barriers would go down further if the masses were
approached to support the National Movement in order to alleviate
their own misery. It cannot entirely be an accident that the Khilafat
and Non-Cooperation Movement (1920–22) was accompanied by scattered, but determined, mass actions against the zamindars on an unprecedented scale: the peasant agitation in Darbhanga, Bihar (1920),
the anti-*taluqdar* peasant riots in Awadh, U.P. (1921–22), and the
Mopla (Mappila) uprising in Malabar, Kerala (1921). Working-class
aspirations too found expression, though a moderate one, in the formation of the All-India Trade Union Congress (AITUC) in 1921, attended by practically all the principal nationalist leaders, except Gandhi.

The new awareness of the necessity of bringing workers and peasants into the National Movement was stressed in C.R. Das's presidential address to the Gaya session of the Congress (1922), and his address
to the AITUC the same year, where he spoke of Swaraj for 'the 98 per
cent'. Gandhi, on his release from prison in 1924, sufficiently shifted

to egalitarianism to demand optional universal suffrage; he now also claimed to be a 'Socialist' in so far as he advocated state ownership of such machine industry as might be permitted in the idyllic India of his vision. In 1925 he gave space in his *Young India* to M.N. Roy, unmindful of British official indignation. Despite Gandhi's opposition, a resolution for condolence on the death of Lenin was lost in the AICC by just 63 votes to 54.[16]

The vote indicated the growth of sympathy for socialism and Soviet Russia in the ranks of the radical sections of the National Movement. From 1923 onwards Jawaharlal Nehru's espousal of 'Independence', replacing the vague concept of Swaraj or Home Rule, drew him to the Communists; and by 1927 his participation in the Communist-led Congress of Oppressed Nationalities at Brussels led to his accepting a position in the newly founded League against Imperialism; and he also visited Soviet Russia. At the close of this year, along with Subhas Bose, he sponsored a successful resolution at the Madras Congress demanding complete Independence; and in 1928 both of them helped to found the Independence for India League. In 1934–35 Nehru wrote of his having 'long been drawn to socialism and communism', and spoke of how 'Marxism lighted up many a dark corner of my mind'. He was obviously speaking of his experience of the late 1920s.[17] A similar inclination towards socialism was found among the 'revolutionaries'. Already in March 1926 Bhagat Singh's attachment to socialism was clear when he founded the Naujiwan Bharat Sabha; and in 1928 when revolutionary groups from all over the country met at Delhi under the leadership of Chandrashekhar Azad and Bhagat Singh, they rechristened their organization as the Hindustan Socialist Republican Army.

These trends must be regarded as having genuine socialist elements within them, and many of M.N. Roy's criticisms of these groups during this period, often sharply expressed, must be regarded as the products of a far too demanding attitude towards those who, by Lenin's definition, were basically bourgeois democrats.[18] Yet it was initially from their ranks that the founders of the Communist movement within the country came.

Communists and National Movement, 1922–29

By 1922 Muzaffar Ahmad in Calcutta, S.A. Dange in Bombay, M. Singaravelu Chettiar in Madras and Ghulam Husain in Lahore had begun, in varying degrees, to spread Communist ideas. The formation of the Swaraj Party undoubtedly suggested the notion of a left-wing party within the National Movement. In 1922 Dange floated the idea of an 'Indian Socialist Labour Party of the Indian National Congress'; the next year Chettiar published a manifesto of the Labour and Kisan Party of Hindustan. In April 1923 Ghulam Husain, editor of *Inquilab*, Lahore, proposed a conference at Lucknow to form a Labour Peasant Party of India. But before these efforts could bear fruit, the British Government arrested the leading Communists and arrayed them in the Cawnpore Bolshevik Conspiracy Case. In May 1924 Muzaffar Ahmad, Shaukat Usmani, Dange and Nalini Gupta were sentenced to four years' rigorous imprisonment. Chettiar 'was exempted from trial only owing to ill-health'.[19] These heavy punishments, as those of the Peshawar cases, drew no perceptible protest from the rest of the nationalist camp – a curious attitude of indifference to civil liberty, if not the cause of national freedom. This fact is one among many which present-day critics of subsequent Communist hostility to moderate nationalism tend entirely to ignore.[20]

In spite of the Cawnpore Conspiracy Case, two developments took place which were to strengthen Left elements considerably. One was the conference of Indian Communists at Cawnpore (Kanpur) itself, held openly in December 1925 at the invitation of a local 'National' Communist, Satyabhakta. The conference elected M. Singaravelu as President and Janaki Prasad Bagerhatta, a member of the AICC, as General Secretary, and put Muzaffar Ahmad (released from prison owing to serious illness), S.Y. Ghate and others on its executive committee. The defiantly open attempt to organize the conference was matched by the resolution of solidarity with thirteen named Communist victims of the Peshawar and Cawnpore cases. The definition of the Party's 'Object' in its constitution was framed without equivocation in the following words:

the establishment of a workers' and peasants' republic based on the socialization of the means of production and distribution, by *the liberation of India from British imperialist domination.*

In a significant statement on the declaration form, it was added:

No one who is a member of any communal organization shall be admitted as a member of the Communist Party.[21]

The Communist Party was, perhaps, the first political party of any significance to exclude persons belonging to communal organizations from its ranks.

The second important development was the formation of a broader-based Left-oriented party in Bengal just preceding the Communist conference at Cawnpore in November 1925: this was 'The Labour Swaraj Party of the Indian National Congress', which in 1926 was renamed the 'Peasants and Workers Party of Bengal'. Its initial inspiration came from left Swarajists like Hemantakumar Sarkar and the revolutionary poet Nazrul Islam; Muzaffar Ahmad worked as the editor of its organ *Langal.* The Party called for 'complete independence of India, based on economic and social emancipation', and, while popularizing Communist ideas, the *Langal* was especially stout-hearted in expressing solidarity with Subhas Bose incarcerated in Mandalay jail since 1924. It also took up issues of peasant rights, and began organizing workers. With it as the model, the Bombay Workers and Peasants Party was founded in January 1927, and, with similar parties formed in U.P. and the Punjab, an all-India Workers and Peasants Party was constituted in December 1928. A universal feature of these parties was the participation at all levels of Congressmen, along with Communists. The new Party's strength was shown on 30 December 1928, when about 20,000 industrial workers marched on the Congress *pandal* at Calcutta demanding that the Congress, then in session, should pass a resolution for complete independence, and reject the goal of Dominion Status adopted in the Motilal Nehru report. They were welcomed and addressed by Jawaharlal Nehru. Nehru also had presided on 27 December at a Socialist Youth Congress at which Communism was declared 'the (only) way out'.

Meerut Repression and Civil Disobedience, 1929–34

Ground was thus clearly being laid for cooperation between the radical nationalist elements and the Communists when the British Government, anxiously watching the growth of this cooperation, struck.[22] On 20 March 1929, thirty-one persons, including practically all important Communist and Left-inclined trade union leaders, were arrested in different parts of the country and brought to Meerut to stand trial, for entering 'into a conspiracy to deprive the King [of England] of the sovereignty of British India'. Two more were added later to be arrested and tried. Three of the Meerut accused were British Communists, including Ben Bradley.[23] The trial dragged on till January 1933, when harsh judgments were pronounced: Muzaffar Ahmad received transportation for life; five, including Dange and Spratt, 12 years; Bradley, Mirajkar and Usmani, 10 years; the remaining seventeen, 4 to 7 years. The heavy sentences were reduced on appeal in August 1933; but even by the end of 1933, Ahmad, Dange, Spratt and Usmani were still in prison. On 23 July 1934, the British Government declared the Communist Party and all its organizations 'unlawful', and their membership a criminal offence.[24]

The Meerut Conspiracy Case deprived the Indian Communist movement of its leadership for full four years (1929–33) and more. It occurred on the eve of the Congress launching its Civil Disobedience Movement immediately after its Lahore session at the end of December 1930, a session made further memorable by Nehru's open espousal of socialism in his presidential address. While, by the Meerut trial, the British Government succeeded in neutralizing Communists and breaking up the Communist-led Workers and Peasants Party, the more radical national elements were won over by the Congress leadership through its new mass movement. Under constant repression, the Communists could not even restore a centralized leadership; the Bombay and Calcutta Communists functioned separately, and in 1932 even the Bombay group split up. M.N. Roy's return in late 1930 and his attempt to form a rival Communist Party further destabilized the Communist ranks. Immediately after the 1929 arrests, Motilal Nehru had chaired, and Jawaharlal Nehru had joined, a committee for the defence of the Meerut accused; but the Congress enthusiasm on their behalf soon waned, especially after the Delhi Statement of 2 November 1929 issued in praise of Lord Irwin and signed by Gandhi, the two Nehrus and other Congress leaders. Neither Bhagat Singh and his comrades (soon to face death sentences) nor the Meerut accused specifically figured in Gandhi's Eleven Points, that were declared to be the basis of Civil Disobedience in 1930; nor were the two groups of prisoners brought within the ambit of the Gandhi–Irwin Agreement of 4 March 1931.

Under the circumstances, the new position taken by the Comintern after its sixth Congress at Moscow, closing on 1 September 1928, could not but find ready response from the embittered ranks of Indian Communists. In line with the rather sectarian assessments of that Congress in general, the Comintern now held Indian 'bourgeois nationalism' to have 'already betrayed the agrarian revolution' and to be 'likely to play a counter-revolutionary role' in future. The 'first task' of the Indian Communists was to form a strong Communist Party, and the 'second' to 'unfold the agrarian revolution' under its leadership, thereby breaking the alliance of 'the imperialists, landlords and the compromising bourgeoisie'.[25] It followed from this that any political alliance with the Congress was not to be thought of. Nor was the Workers and Peasants Party (WPP), a 'dual'-class party of a type expressly endorsed by Stalin in 1925, now thought deserving of so much attention as had been paid to it by the Communists at the cost of building their own party.[26] The latter advice was easy to follow, since, with the jailing of the Communist leaders at Meerut, the WPP could hardly function and practically died a natural death. As for the warnings about trusting the Congress, these too fell on receptive ears among Indian Communists. The Delhi Statement of the Congress leaders of 2 November 1929, which tormented Jawaharlal Nehru's conscience,[27] and the termination of the Civil Disobedience Movement in 'a whimper', in Nehru's own description,[28] drew much scorn. When Gandhi addressed a 'labour meeting' at Parel, Bombay, on 16 March 1931, to explain his agreement with Irwin, Communist hecklers taunted him for forgetting the Meerut accused, his own Eleven Points and 'the substance of Independence'.[29] In their defence statements the Meerut accused strongly criticized Gandhiji's subsequent participation in the Second Round Table Conference in London in 1931, and his compromising stance there. The bitterness went so far that in Calcutta in 1934, the Communists helped to organize a 'League against Gandhism'.[30]

In his *Autobiography* Nehru sums up in a few pages, what appeared to him in 1934–35 to be the position of the 'orthodox Communists'. As one may expect, he dismisses as 'fantastic' the Communists' belief that the Congress leaders, tied to the capitalists and landlords, 'do not want the British to go away'. He, however, does admit that 'many of their [Communists'] theoretical criticisms were able and pointed and subsequent events partly justified them'.[31]

Socialists and Other Left Forces in Congress, 1930–34

The Civil Disobedience Movement, in so far as it brought large masses into the National Movement for the first time, quickened the ger-mination of socialist and Left ideas within the Congress, at the same time as the concessions and compromises occurred on the part of the national leadership. Nehru held in 1934–35 that 'some people in the Congress, and they are a growing number, want to change the land system, and the capitalist system', though 'they cannot speak in the name of the Congress'.[32] The claim was not baseless. Nehru had him-self done much to further the spread of socialist ideas; and at the Karachi Congress in March 1931, he drafted and Gandhi introduced a Resolu-tion on Fundamental Rights which promised substantial rent and debt reduction, and the state's control of key industries and ownership of mineral resources, along with promises of such 'bourgeois–demo-cratic rights' as universal suffrage, equality for women and abolition of caste disabilities.[33] It was elaborated and made into a full-scale programme by the AICC in August 1931. By and large, it could serve as a 'minimum' programme for the Left as well.

In July 1931 Jaya Prakash Narayan helped found the Socialist Party, whose counterparts were established in other provinces in the next few years, mainly by those working in the Congress. These groups coalesc-ed into an All-India *Congress* Socialist Party (CSP) in 1934, its mem-bers ranging from avowed Marxists like Narayan and Narendra Dev to supporters of the British Labour Party like Minoo Masani. They were drawn initially to M.N. Roy, who having returned from his exile after his expulsion from the Comintern, was arguing that Communists should work within the Congress, and by so doing, bring about a change in its leadership.[34] The significant growth in the influence of the CSP within the Congress was another sign that there was considerable potential for the acceptance of socialist ideas in its ranks; and this could not but help bring about a change in the Communists' attitude towards the Congress.

Towards 'National Front', 1936–37

From the 1929 Meerut arrests onwards the Communists were faced with a persecution in which there was hardly any let-up until 1933.[35] Just being a Communist was itself an act of 'civil disobedience', though it may not have been ever so called. Despite their formal disavowal of the Gandhi-led Civil Disobedience as being far too limited and passive, a number of Communists, such as S.G. Sardesai, went to jail as Satyagrahis; and other Communists such as Bankim Mukherji, Abdur Razzaq Khan and Moni Singh received severely heavy sentences for agitational activities against the government.[36] The Communists' position in the trade unions was weakened not only by repression, but also by the economic crisis of 1929–32 and growing unemployment, which made working-class response to strike calls increasingly tepid. The Moderates split away from the AITUC in 1929 (with Nehru supporting the Communist position); and in the rump AITUC there was another split in 1931, with Communists now seceding to form the 'Red TUC'.[37]

In such circumstances, the exhortations made to Indian Communists in the Three Parties' (Chinese, British, German) Letter of 1932 and the Chinese Party's letter of 1933, to build their Party and take the lead in powerful anti-imperialist actions, independently and on their own, were surely unrealistic. But the letters did recommend a greater resort to the united-front strategy, and a re-unification of the trade unions. To this extent they were certainly a helpful factor in the Communist Party's partial recovery.[38]

The situation began to change with 1933, when most of the Meerut prisoners were released, following reductions of their sentences on appeal. The fragmented groups were reunited, and a provisional Central Committee of the Communist Party formed. By late 1934 much revival had taken place, and the Party's work in trade unions was spreading; contacts had been made too with the newly formed Congress Socialist Party (CSP), within which some Communists (like Ajoy Ghosh and P. Sundarayya) had begun to work. The controversy with the followers of M.N. Roy (himself the victim of a harsh sentence given out at Cawnpore, and in prison till 1936) no longer prevented common action with the Royists in the trade unions, leading, in 1935, to the return of the Communists to the AITUC. All these were creditable achievements made in the face of the Government's ban imposed on the Communist Party and its organizations in July 1934, and of regular cycles of imprisonment to which Communists remained subject.

'National Front', 1935–37

It was during this phase of recovery that the Seventh Congress of the Comintern met in August 1935 at Moscow. Recognizing the emergence of fascism as a world-wide phenomenon of extreme danger, especially after Hitler's rise to power in Germany in 1933, G. Dimitrov, in his report to the Congress, called for an extensive 'people's united front', which was to include Social Democrats and other anti-fascist forces.[39] As a corollary to this, Wang Ming, in his report on the colonial countries at the same Congress, asked Indian Communists not to 'disregard work within the National Congress', in effect treating the Congress as a genuine part of the anti-imperialist united front. The specific implications were worked out in an important article ('The Anti-Imperialist People's Front in India') by R. Palme Dutt and Ben Bradley(of the British Communist Party), which came to be known as the Dutt–Bradley theses (February 1936).[40]

The theses contained the following major propositions. (1) The most broad-based unity was desirable on the basis of (a) 'a line of consistent struggle against imperialism', and (b) 'struggle for the vital needs of the toiling masses'. (2) The Congress was 'the principal existing mass organization of many diverse elements seeking national liberation'. (3) Several previous actions of the Congress leadership had been 'disastrous' and 'equivalent to surrender to imperialism'. (4) There was thus need to criticize the Congress leadership, but only with the purpose of assisting the Congress to play its true role, and not to weaken the unity of the elements already in the Congress. (5) The Congress had the potential 'by the further transformation of its organization and programme' to 'become the form of realization of the Anti-Imperialist People's Front'. (6) 'Mass organizations of workers and peasants', of youth, etc., should be developed and their affiliation to the Congress striven for. (7) Democratization of the Congress (e.g., elected Working Committee) should be demanded. (8) A minimum programme should be presented to the Congress, based on 'complete independence', civil liberty (including right to strike), repeal of repressive laws, release of political prisoners, protection of rights of workers (including 8-hour day), 50 per cent rent reduction for peasants and security from seizure of their lands by landlords and moneylenders. (9) The question of whether 'Non-violence' should be a requisite dogma for the Congress should be raised, but the issue 'should not be allowed to split the national front'. (10) There should be a consolidation of the left-wing comprising 'Congress Socialists, Trade Unionists, Communists and Left Congressmen', in which 'the Congress Socialist Party (CSP) can play an especially important part'. (11) The Left Wing should try to have a number of its candidates run in the ensuing elections (under the Act of 1935), while preventing 'a splitting of the National Front [votes] in the elections'. (12) The slogan of a Constituent Assembly to make free India's own constitution was to be presented as a central slogan.

The Dutt–Bradley theses were rapidly accepted by the Indian Communists, and began to bear fruit almost immediately.[41] Already under the influence of the Seventh Comintern Congress, the CSP National Executive, meeting at Meerut in January 1936, had decided to withdraw its earlier formal ban on Communists' entry into the CSP, originally imposed in 1934, and henceforward Communists were allowed to seek admission to CSP on an individual basis.[42] Communists thereupon began to enter the CSP from April 1936 onwards; and this gave them effectual entry into the Congress as well.

When the Congress met for its general session at Lucknow in April 1936, once again under the presidentship of Jawaharlal Nehru, the Left was able to make its presence felt in a significant manner. Nehru spoke of socialism, of the need for 'ending private property, except in a restricted sense', and of 'the new civilization' represented by the resurgent Soviet Union. Though the Left-sponsored resolutions for affiliation of mass organizations, rejection of ministerial office after elections under the 1935 Act and a proportionally elected Working Committee were rejected, the votes in favour were respectable in number.[43] Nehru included three CSP leaders in the Working Committee (including J.P. Narayan) for the first time. Simultaneously, the All-India Kisan Congress (afterwards, Sabha) and the Progressive Writers' Association were founded at conferences held in Lucknow about the same time.[44] In both these organizations, the Communists rapidly became the main force, rallying peasants and writers behind the National Movement, while also expanding their own ideological influence. The Royists and Communists in the AITUC achieved conciliation with the right-wing National TU Federation, though the expected merger at the Nagpur session of AITUC in 1936 did not take place; it came two years later.

The spurt in the mass-hold of the Left that followed is indicated by the expansion in the membership of the All-India Kisan Sabha (AIKS) and the rising tide of the strike movement. By the time of its congress at Camilla (Bengal) in May 1938, the membership of the All-India Kisan Sabha (AIKS) had crossed half a million; by its Gaya congress in April 1939, it had reached 8,00,000. In 1938 the AIKS adopted the red flag for its banner. As for the working days lost through industrial disputes, an index of militant trade union strength, these had fallen to below 1 million in 1935, but now climbed to 2.4 million in 1936, almost 9 million in 1937 and above 9 million in 1938.[45] When the Congress ministries took office in eight out of eleven provinces in 1937, the ban on the Communist Party ceased in practice to be implemented, and this too helped the Communists to expand their areas of influence.

The National Front in Crisis, 1938–39

The growth in the mass influence of the Left found its reflection in the increasing strength of the Left within the Congress, especially the AICC. When the Congress began preparing for the 1937 elections, the election manifesto endorsed at the Faizpur Congress (December 1936) was based on the Karachi Resolution and had a manifestly Left orientation. In 1939 there were twenty avowed Communists in the AICC within the much larger CSP contingent of AICC members. Communist influence within the CSP was on the rise as well, with E.M.S.

Namboodiripad and Sajjad Zaheer becoming joint secretaries of the CSP. The greatest triumph of the Left was the re-election of Subhas Bose as Congress President early in 1939. Subhas Bose had been a radical Congress leader who had for long suffered for his views. His earlier fascination with fascism now seemed to be a past chapter, and, succeeding Nehru as President of the Congress in 1938, he continued the left-leaning policy of his predecessor. In January 1939 he decided to seek re-election, and, confronting Gandhi's own candidate Sita-ramayya, won by 1,580 votes to 1,375. Newspapers proclaimed it a victory of the Left, and it may be regarded as the high tide of its influence in the Congress.

The triumph proved to be short-lived, however. As early as 1934 Gandhi had declared socialist ideas to be 'distasteful' to him; and though he admitted that the socialists had a right to be represented in the Congress, he declared it unacceptable that they should 'gain ascendancy' there. As the Left grew within the Congress, Gandhi's sympathies with the right-wing became more open, though he took care to nurse his relationship with Nehru, who to many appeared to be the leading figure on the left side. When the Congress opted for elections and ministries, the work of choosing candidates and controlling ministries was left to a parliamentary board with Vallabhbhai Patel as chairman, and Azad and Rajendra Prasad as the other members – a purely right-wing body. There were few Leftists chosen as candidates and the support to even a single AITUC candidate (K.N. Joglekar) was refused, leading to Dange's resignation from the Congress.[46] Once the Congress ministries were formed, the CSP refused to join them, with the result that the Congress ministries were mainly dominated by representatives of the right-wing. (It is now a matter to be considered whether such self-denial was a correct decision on the part of the Left.)

Once the ministries began to function, the tension between them and the Left-led mass organizations, notably the Kisan Sabha and the AITUC, became increasingly sharper. The crisis came in Bihar: the famous peasant leader Sahajanand resigned from the working committee of the Bihar PCC to free himself for leading peasants' struggles against a government that was so openly supportive of the landlords. Even Nehru joined Gandhi and the right in expressing suspicions that the Kisan Sabhas were undermining the Congress organization. In

September 1938 Gandhi proposed a 'purge' of the Congress, clearly aimed at the Left; and the Delhi AICC during the same month asked Congress ministries to act strongly against those who pursued 'class war by violent means'. About the same time, acting under the influence of the mill-owners, the Bombay government introduced the Bombay Industrial Disputes Bill against which the trade unions unitedly organized a general strike on 7 November 1938.[47]

Those conflicts led to increasingly sour relations between the Left and the right, which enabled Subhas Bose to mobilize support for his electoral victory ahead of the Tripuri session of the Congress (March 1939). But the Communists as well as the Socialists were not prepared for a total break with the right, for such a break would have meant the end of the National Front. Thus when the right moved a resolution at Tripuri to bind Bose to the 'wishes' of Gandhiji, the CSP and the Communists tried to avoid a split by not opposing the resolution. Subhas Bose, faced with non-cooperation from both Gandhi and Nehru, resigned. Thereafter he and his followers, organized in the Forward Bloc, were isolated (despite a short-lived Left Coordination Committee consisting of the Forward Bloc, Royists, CSP and Communists), and were hounded out of the Congress on disciplinary grounds after July 1939.

Under the pressure of the right, the unity of the Left began to break still further. M.N. Roy could have justifiably maintained that his argument for working through the Congress had in part anticipated the 'tactical line' approved at the 7th Congress of the Comintern; but he now shifted increasingly to the right, asking his followers to resign from the CSP in 1937 and opposing the Kisan Sabha. After witnessing the fate of Bose's followers, the CSP leadership became afraid of suffering a similar fate, and began a purge of the Communists after Masani, Lohia and others pressed the issue in May 1939. By May next year the Communists had been expelled; but the result was a loss of very large CSP membership, the CSPs in Andhra (led by P. Sundarayya and Rajeswara Rao) and Kerala (led by E.M.S. Nambodiripad and A.K. Gopalan) practically turning into provincial units of the Communist Party.[48] The Communists gained control of the leadership of the major mass organizations, the AITUC, AIKS and the All-India Students Federation, hitherto regarded as being under CSP influence.

Though the Communist Party now emerged as the major force

among all the groups of the Left, the anti-imperialist 'national front' was certainly gravely weakened by the dissensions. And these dissensions, we must remember, came clearly from the right's firm resolve to risk everything in order to stem the rising influence of the radical forces.[49]

From Imperialist War to People's War, 1939–42

When World War II broke out on 3 September 1939, opinion in the Indian National Movement was divided: on the one side was the antipathy to the British as masters of India, on the other, hostility to the Nazis as upholders of everything offensive to human dignity. The Congress ministries were directed by the party's high command to resign, because the British Government had made India a belligerent country without consulting the representatives of the Indian people. Direct rule was thereupon proclaimed in the Congress-ruled provinces. The Congress nevertheless offered to cooperate with the British Government in its pursuit of war, if some substantive concessions were given. These offers were met by vague promises as in the Viceroy's statement of 17 October 1939 and in his 'August Offer' of 8 August 1940. Such responses fortified the view that the empire was what the war was about, and concessions would not, therefore, be made at its cost. The Congress leadership was compelled to begin 'an individual civil disobedience campaign' under Gandhiji's leadership from October 1940. The Government replied by large-scale arrests; and by May 1941 some 20,000 were in prison.

The Communist Party, in line with the Comintern positions,[50] treated the war as an 'inter-imperialist' war, having been preceded by the Munich conspiracy (1938) and the Soviet response thereto through its Non-Aggression Pact with Germany (1939). This being so, it was essential that the 'National Front' policy should be continued in the interest of opposing 'one's own' imperialist power. A restoration of the old Left unity was no longer possible because of the increasing anti-Soviet stance of the CSP leadership. With Subhas Bose some relations continued to be maintained, and there is evidence that individual Communists were involved in his escape from India to the Soviet Union in the summer of 1940.[51] At the same time, with the imposition of direct British rule after the exit of the Congress ministries, the Communists became subject to the 1934 ban, and their hide-and-seek with arrests and imprisonments began once again. By May 1941 almost the entire Communist leadership was in jail, along with a very large number of the Party's 5,000 membership. The result of all this was, as the General Secretary of the Party, P.C. Joshi, was to note in 1942, that though 'the National Front remain[ed] intact ... it did not move forward'.[52] There could be doubt, too, whether it was really 'intact', except from the side of the Communists.

Nazi Germany launched its attack on the Soviet Union on 22 June 1941. This brought about a change in the complexion of the war; but unlike other Communist parties, the Indian Communist leadership, most of it in prison, found it difficult to turn away from the long-established position of hostility to British imperialism, and to begin to treat it as an ally in a world-wide coalition. There were naturally overtures from the British Communist Party for a change in Communist policy, an article from R.P. Dutt, 'A Policy for the Indian People', appearing in October 1941. At last, Communist leaders held in the Deoli camp prepared their 'Jail Document' in December, in which they argued forcefully for a change of policy to one of 'People's War'.[53] The entry of Japan in the war in the same month and its quick successes in South-East Asia brought India closer to the theatres of war, and made the shift of policy still more urgent.

There was already a similar shift of position in the Congress leadership. The British Government was compelled to release the principal Congress leaders in December 1941, whereafter they met at Bardoli to pass a resolution noting 'the new world situation which has arisen in the war and its approach to India', and offering to join the Allies ('United Nations') on behalf of 'a free and independent India'. The resolution, ratified by the Congress, prepared the ground for the Cripps Mission (March–April) which offered dominion status, with power to secede from the empire, a Constituent Assembly, self-determination for provinces, minority protection – but all after the War. For the moment the transfer would be withheld. The negotiations with the Congress broke down on the last issue.

It was from this point that the Congress leadership, without expressly reneging from their animosity to Germany and Japan, shifted to a policy of confrontation with the British Government, leading to the 'Quit-India' resolution of the AICC (8 August 1942). The Communists' opposition to the resolution secured only 13 votes in the AICC. Their case rested on the pre-eminent need to defeat the Axis powers, and thus invoked the call of internationalism. Jawaharlal Nehru admitted that in Gandhi's pressing on for a new movement against British authority, 'nationalism had triumphed over internationalism'.[54] It seems that with the Germans seemingly poised to break through the Soviet defences on the Volga, and the British empire menaced on the borders of Egypt by Germany and on India's eastern frontier by the Japanese, Gandhiji felt that the British, as part of a seriously endangered coalition, could soon be compelled to come to terms with the Congress.[55] The resolution itself stated that the Congress was 'anxious not to embarrass in any way the defence of China and Russia'; and Nehru tells us that both Gandhi and Azad (as President) in their final speeches stressed 'a desire for settlement' and contemplated negotiations, rather than immediate action.[56] It was the British Government that precipitated matters by carrying out large-scale arrests and then violently suppressing spontaneous protests against the arrests. In an ironical twist to events, the Red Army's historic victory at Stalingrad in the winter of 1942–43 freed the British Government from any anxiety over the safety of its empire and so giving in to any Indian demands under the pressures of war. This ruled out any immediate gains coming to India out of the Quit-India Movement.

The Communists' opposition to the Quit-India resolution was made the reason for their post-war expulsion (1945) from the Congress, and the issue has been raised at various times since then to question their patriotism; but there is no doubt that, if one concedes that the defeat of Fascism was the primary need of the world at that hour, then the position the Communists adopted was unexceptionable.

United Front for People's War, 1942–45

The Communist Party's position, after its legalization on 22 July 1942 (for which there had to be negotiations with the British Government) and the passage of the Quit-India resolution, left it the only Party out of the old National Front which was not facing repression. Its position with regard to the British Government, while not confrontationist, was independent. It never relented on its demand for the release of Congress prisoners and formation of a national government. The Party's central committee's resolution of 19 September 1942 demanded that the British government agree:

> to stop this [post-Quit India] offensive of repression against the people and the Congress, to release Mahatma Gandhi and the Congress leaders, to lift the ban on the Congress and to open negotiations for the establishment of Provisional National Government.

The Communists strongly rejected a proposal by Amery, the British Secretary of State for India, for a coalition of non-Congress parties (*People's War* editorial, 18 October 1942).

The Communists thus opposed both the Congress's decision to go in for non-cooperation and the British Government's provocative policy of repression. These were political positions: in practice the Communists avoided open cooperation with British officialdom,[57] built up trade unions and Kisan Sabha organizations, and fought in a restrained manner for the people's day-to-day demands and reliefs. In the situation they became practically the sole legal spokesmen for the common man. While a 'no-strike' policy was declared, campaigns were organized against hoarders and for proper food distribution; and 'grow more food' campaigns, appealing directly to peasants, were also attempted. Relief activities were organized, the most important being those during the Bengal famine of 1943–44. Mass work of this nature, combined with a large circulation of Marxist literature (the ban against it having been removed), resulted in a very considerable growth of the Communist Party. In June 1945, a secret official report estimated the Party's membership at 30,000 (up from 5,000 in 1942) and its trade-union following at a quarter of a million. It now published ten weekly journals, and its main organ, *People's War*, had a circulation of 25,000 to 30,000 copies. The same report notes increasing Communist influence among students; and, it might have added, peasants.[58]

These gains had to be set by the side of the Party's isolation from practically all the segments that had comprised the 'National Front' of the late 1930s. The bulk of the Congress was estranged by the refusal of the Communists to follow, in Nehru's words, 'the national forces in whatever they are doing', i.e., the Quit-India movement.[59] Particularly bitter were the relations with the erstwhile Left allies, the CSP, whom the Communists now regarded as 'saboteurs' for harming the cause of people's war by their resort to violence against British authority, and the 'Forward Bloc', whose workers were deemed potential 'traitors' for their support of Subhas Bose, now trying to assemble the INA in collaboration with Japan. As for M.N. Roy, regarded as a 'renegade' even in the best of times, he fulfilled expectations by moving over entirely to the British side. Such isolation impending even before the Quit-India resolution inspired a new version of the National Front; this was to be a Congress–Muslim League alliance, in friendly cooperation with the Communist Party. The first important statement of the new position came in an article, 'National Unity Now', published in *People's War* on the very day of the Quit-India resolution.[60]

We should remember that the Communist position on the communal problem up till now had been practically indistinguishable from that of the Congress Left. As early as 1928, the Communist-led Workers and Peasants Party, while accepting 'the solution proposed to the communal question' by the All-parties' Report (rejected by M.A Jinnah), had argued that the question hardly merited 'such excessive amount of attention', since 'experience tends to show that there is little communal feeling among the masses'.[61] Alternatively, it was thought that communalism would wither away as the people's economic demands were achieved through common struggles. The Muslim League was not considered a suitable party in which Communists should work: Hasrat Mohani had been expelled for that reason. In 1937–38 the Communists were active in the Muslim Mass Contact campaign of the Congress, which immediately provoked bitter opposition from the Muslim League.

It was now argued by Adhikari that conditions had changed. Ever since the Muslim League's campaign against the alleged ill-treatment of Muslims under the Congress ministries, the League's influence among Muslims had grown enormously; and with the Lahore resolution of 1940, which became the basis for the Pakistan demand, the League had made Partition a necessary element of any further constitutional development acceptable to it. With due encouragement from, and collaboration with, the British Government (which, for example, made minority League ministries possible in NWFP and Assam), the League was meeting little organized ideological or political opposition from the Congress, whose leadership, at all levels, remained incarcerated for the larger part of the War period.[62] Clearly, once the League had grown in strength, there had to be negotiations with it; and to this extent, Communist proposals that the Congress and League leaderships should come together, and certain concessions be given to the League as a party, were unexceptionable. This was a position which the Congress in fact adopted from the Gandhi–Jinnah talks of 1944 onwards.

But Adhikari's article and subsequent CPI policy statements went much further than this. It was held that the Muslim League had undergone a transformation: since 1938 it had become the spokesman of the 'anti-imperialist sentiment' of the Muslim petty-bourgeois masses; and the League leadership had been transformed from a 'feudal reactionary' to an 'industrial bourgeois leadership', playing an 'oppositional role vis-a-vis imperialism'. In effect, therefore, the class character and anti-imperialist credentials of the League were equated with those of the Congress. The two parties were asked to come together in a new 'national unity'. For such unity the previous Congress programme of freedom of religious worship and protection of minorities was insufficient. The Congress must agree to the right of self-determination; it was 'just and right' in the Pakistan demand that 'nationalities', such as those of Sindhis, Baluchis, Pathans and Punjabi Muslims, should have the right to secede. In a further report (September 1942), Adhikari invoked the Marxist–Leninist positions on national self-determination, especially quoting Stalin's 1925 reference to the 'scores of hitherto unknown nationalities, having their own separate languages and separate cultures, [that] will appear on the scene' in India 'in the event of a revolutionary upheaval'.[63] This was now to be often quoted in justification of the Pakistan demand, though the fact that Stalin had never contemplated a religious nationality arising out of a linguistic one (e.g., Punjabi Muslim, or Bengali Muslim) was simply glossed over.[64]

This theoretical position ('the Adhikari thesis'), which was confirmed in comparatively cautious language by the political resolution of CPI's first congress in May 1943,[65] had immediate practical implications. Communists (i.e. such as were Muslims) were now to work in the League, as they had done in the Congress. They were expected to spread progressive ideas in the League ranks; and in June (May?) 1945, Z.A.

Ahmad, perhaps on this basis, was assuring Jawaharlal Nehru of 'the rapidity with which popular forces are growing in the League'.[66] How the 'nationality' fig-leaf could slip is shown by the fact that in the 1946 elections the Communist Party decided to support 'the League against all rivals [i.e. including Congress]' in 'all those Muslim seats' in which the CPI's own candidates were not contesting, irrespective of whether the seats were in the areas of the so-called 'Muslim nationalities' of the North-West or anywhere else in India.[67] Everywhere, therefore, the Communists and their supporters would be divided among Muslims and non-Muslims. Such a situation was disastrous for the growth of progressive ideas among Muslims; and in fact a number of Communists and progressive people working in the League at the Party's behest were now permanently lost to the Communist movement.

It was, perhaps, merely a logical extension of the Adhikari thesis that in December 1945, the Party released a scheme for a 'Sikh homeland', thus further dividing the Punjab into three nationalities.[68] Fortunately this was a much briefer aberration than the pursuit of Pakistan.

Anti-Imperialist and Anti-Communal Struggle, 1945–47

As World War II drew to a close and the fall of the Axis powers became a matter of time, it became obvious that Communists must shift from the strategy of people's war back to the strategy of anti-imperialist struggle. In December 1945 the CPI Central Committee described 'the post-war period in India' as 'the period of unprecedented opportunity to make the final bid for power'.[69] The moral and material strength of imperialism had greatly suffered owing to the successes of the Red Army, the detachment of East European states from the imperialist system, the strength of the People's Liberation Army in China, the armed struggle for independence in South-East Asia and, not the least, a great erosion of the grip of imperialism on the popular mind in the metropolitan countries. There was, therefore, every justification for showing a greater degree of militancy in the fight against British rule in India. Since there was now a return to the established Marxist view that the landlords and princes were inextricably linked with imperialism and the bourgeoisie was prone to compromises ('an alliance between British big business and their Indian brothers' was thought to be impending), the national agitations could be accompanied by economic struggles of workers and peasants (the period of 'no strike' being declared to be over). In this the role of the Communists was emphasized by speaking of the United National Front of this phase as that of 'Congress–League–Communist Unity' instead of just 'Congress–League Unity'.[70] The Communist Party showed its mettle considerably in the agitation over the INA trials. Putting aside its opposition to the INA during the People's War period, it treated INA men as fighters for freedom in line with the general national sentiment. Students' strikes were combined with industrial strikes in February 1946. Almost simultaneously came the RIN mutiny (18–23 February) at Bombay: Congress, League and Communist flags went up on the naval ships and establishments. An industrial strike called by the Communists in sympathy with the ratings paralysed Bombay; and hundreds were killed in clashes with British troops and police. These events have an indelible place in the annals of the National Movement, since they helped immeasurably to bring independence closer.

The Communist-led economic struggles were also intensified. The Tebhaga movement in Bengal, initiated in 1944 to reduce the rent to a third of the produce, spread to many parts of Bengal during the subsequent three years. In 1944–46 there were strikes by the tribal Warlis in Maharashtra against forced labour, high rents and usury. A sharper political character was assumed by the coir and other workers' movement in Travancore–Cochin: in a state-wide strike in October 1946, army firing claimed lives of hundreds of the volunteers, now known from the two places concerned as the Punnapra–Vayalar martyrs. In July 1946 began the great uprising of the Telengana peasants against the Nizam and the landlords, which was to continue till 1951, constituting the greatest armed struggle of the peasantry in Indian history.[71] The Communists also participated in the Quit-Kashmir movement of Shaikh Abdullah's National Conference (May 1946).

These actions, with some exceptions (INA agitations and Quit-Kashmir), were entirely under Communist leadership, unsupported by the Congress or the Muslim League. The Congress leadership was interested in negotiating for freedom on the strength of its massive support among the Indian people. The Muslim League just concentrated on its slogan of Pakistan. The 1946 elections (on restricted franchise) led to a situation in which the Congress dominated the 'general', and the League, the 'Muslim' constituencies; the Communists polled just 2.5 per cent of the vote in the Provincial Assembly elections. The plans and counterplans that emerged from the Simla Conference and the Cabinet Mission (1946) made it increasingly difficult for the CPI to support the Muslim League's positions. It became clear that the League leadership was of the same reactionary hue as before. This was recognized in an important article, 'Freedom for India', by R.P. Dutt (July 1946), when he described the current League leadership as of 'big Muslim land-owners',[72] this being at total variance from Adhikari's description of the same leadership in 1942.The facts on the ground began to demand a reconsideration of the entire question of Pakistan. R.P. Dutt examined the issue with his customary thoroughness in the 1947 edition of *India Today*, and found no justification for the concept of Pakistan on the basis of any theory of nationality.[73] He had apparently put these views earlier in *Labour Monthly* (March 1946), and though initially received with some reserve in the Party,[74] his writings must have begun to exercise their influence in time, being at least partly reflected in a Central Committee resolution of August 1946.[75]

The communal riots that preceded and accompanied the Partition could not demarcate the Congress and League better. Despite the undoubted growth of communal sentiments in the Congress, which the CPI constantly pointed out, Gandhi's valiant fight to protect both Hindus and Muslims from communal slaughter had no counterpart on the League side. The Communists had no large mass influence of a similar kind, but their fight against communalism during this period forms an epic chapter in their contribution to the National Movement: it has seldom received the recognition it deserves.

When the Mountbatten Award was announced, the Party's Central Committee offered to 'fully cooperate with the national leadership [of the Indian Union] in the proud task of building the Indian Republic on democratic foundations'. The programme that it put before the 'national leadership' demanded that there be:

Full protection to religious and cultural rights of Muslims.

No discrimination against Muslims in services or in any other sphere of life. Open repudiation of elements [RSS, etc.] which preach that Muslims are alien inside the Indian Union.[76]

Confronted with the rising communal tide in India and the growing strength of the right-wing headed by Vallabhbhai Patel, the CPI gave its support to Nehru, 'the voice of the people', and called for a front with him and the Socialists (October 1947). The next month, alarmed at the deteriorating situation, the Party offered its cooperation to Nehru again and asked for a 'progressive reorganization of government'. On Gandhi's murder on 30 January 1948, the Communists were foremost among the mourners and firmest in demanding action against the communal forces.

This phase naturally closed, as after Independence (15 August 1947) the Nehru Government stabilized, and the larger issues of struggle against the big bourgeoisie, landlords and the remnants of imperialist control presented themselves. At the Party's Calcutta Congress in March 1948, a new radical line was charted under B.T. Ranadive who had replaced P.C. Joshi as General Secretary. In a sense this reflected the need to adjust to the new situation, where, the National Movement having mainly fulfilled its objectives, a new policy had to be framed.

Thus when Independence came, but power went to the propertied classes with much imperialist influence remaining, the Communists resolved to continue the struggle for attaining the full vision of a free India that the united National Movement had promised to the Indian people. The continuation of the struggle tended to cloud the memory of the contribution they had themselves made to achieve national freedom. It is, therefore, all the more necessary to put the record straight, and to recall the sacrifices rendered by countless members and friends of the Communist movement as part of the great struggle that ultimately made India free.

Notes

[1] The crucial 1853 article, 'Future Results of British Rule in India', from which I have just quoted, and the entire corpus of writings on India during the 1850s, are brought together in *Karl Marx on India*, edited by Iqbal Husain, New Delhi, 2006, the 1853 article being printed on pp. 46–51.

[2] Edward W. Said, *Orientalism,* New York, 1979, pp. 153–57. Said's reading of Marx turns out to be as limited as his remarks are self-assured. He does not, for example, appear to be aware of Marx's writings on the 1857 Revolt, for which there was absolutely no excuse in the 1970s since these were all published in a Moscow publication of 1959 (Marx and Engels, *The First Indian War of Independence*), and in a 'Western' edition by Shlomo Avineri (in *Karl Marx: On Colonialism and Modernization,* New York, 1968).

[3] Cf. P.C. Joshi and K. Damodaran, *Marx Comes to India,* Delhi, 1975, p. 2.

[4] *Poverty and Un-British Rule in India,* Delhi, 1962, p. 184.

[5] See Marx's letter to N.Y. Danielsen, 19 February 1881, in Marx and Engels, *Selected Correspondence,* Moscow, p. 408; it will also be found in Marx and Engels, *On Colonialism,* 4th enlarged edition, Moscow, 1968, p. 304. Compare Naoroji's statements in his memoranda of 1880, published in *Poverty and Un-British Rule,* pp. 176, 182–83.

[6] William Z. Foster, *History of the Three Internationals,* Vol. I, Delhi, 1956, pp. 216–18.

[7] V.I. Lenin, *Selected Works,* Vol. IV, Lawrence and Wishart, London, 1943, pp. 29 7–304.

[8] One is reminded of Lenin's observation to be made six years later (1914), that 'the bourgeois movement of emancipation in Ireland [when it] grew stronger and assumed revolutionary forms' helped to persuade Karl Marx to take a position of unqualified support for Irish independence ('The Right of Nations to Self Determination', ibid., p. 278).

[9] Ibid., pp. 299–300.

[10] Ibid., p. 278.

[11] Mao Zedong, 'On the People's Democratic Dictatorship', *Selected Works,* Vol. IV, Peking, 1969, p. 413.

[12] The theses are published in Lenin, *Selected Works,* Vol. X, London, 1946, pp. 231–38, and his speech, ibid., pp. 239–44.

[13] All quotations here are from Lenin's speech, op. cit. M.N. Roy's supplementary theses, also adopted by the Comintern, presented a rather more critical view of bourgeois–democratic national aspirations than did Lenin; but, as E.H. Carr observes, these did not command much attention in actual practice (*The Bolshevik Revolution, 1917–23,* Vol. III, Harmondsworth, 1953, pp. 253–60).

[14] J.V. Stalin, *Works,* Vol. VII, Moscow, 1954, p. 151. Stalin had, indeed, called for the formation in the colonies of 'a workers' and peasants' party' representing the bloc of Communists and the revolutionary elements of the petty bourgeoisie (ibid., pp. 149–51). The text is not correctly represented by Aditya Mukherjee, in *Studies in History,* III (1–2), 1981, special issue (hereinafter cited as *The Left in India*), edited by Bipan Chandra, New Delhi, 1981, p. 28 and n., despite the caveat in the footnote.

[15] Bipan Chandra, *The Rise and Growth of Economic Nationalism in India: Economic Policies of Indian National Leadership, 1880–1905,* New Delhi, 1966.

[16] See G. Adhikari (ed.), *Documents of the History of the Communist Party of India*, Vol. II, Delhi, 1974, pp. 431–35.

[17] Jawaharlal Nehru, *An Autobiography*, London, 1942, pp. 362–63.

[18] With this, in 1935, Nehru too concurred: 'The Indian National Movement is obviously not a labour or proletarian movement. It is a *bourgeois* movement, as its very name implies, and its objective has been not a change in the social order, but political independence' *(Autobiography,* p. 366). A more generous view than Roy's was taken by Stalin in 1924, when he spoke of the national movements of 'India and China, every step of which along the road to liberation, even if it runs counter to the demands of formal democracy, is a steam-hammer blow at imperialism, i.e., is undoubtedly a revolutionary step' ('Foundations of Leninism', in J. Stalin, *Works,* Vol. VI, p. 149).

[19] Ghulam Husain apparently accepted conditions as to his future conduct and was released.

[20] E.g., Aditya Mukherjee, in *The Left in India,* edited by Bipan Chandra, pp. 1–40.

[21] G. Adhikari (ed.), *Documents of the Communist Party of India,* Vol. II (1923–25), pp. 661–70.

[22] On 21 February 1929, the Government of India addressed a policy letter to the Provincial Governments voicing the suspicion that 'Congressmen like Jawaharlal Nehru' might enter into 'temporary alliance with Communists, who have been active among the industrial workers of Calcutta and Bombay' (text summarized in Judith M. Brown, *Gandhi and Civil Disobedience,* Cambridge, 1977, p. 60).

[23] For papers preparatory to the Meerut trial, see Subodh Roy, *Communism in India: Unpublished Documents, 1925–1934,* Calcutta, 1972–1980, pp. 89–163. Of Lester Hutchinson, one of the three British prisoners, it is not established that he was formally a member of the British Communist Party.

[24] See ibid., pp. 470–76 and pp. 445–59, for imprisonment of Communists at Ahmedabad in 1935 under the ban.

[25] *Documents of the History of the CPI,* Vol. III(c) (1928), p. 628.

[26] Cf. John Patrick Haithcox, *Communism and Nationalism in India: M.N. Roy and Comintern Policy,* Princeton, 1971, pp. 108–28, for a summary of the Comintern's Sixth Congress debates on the question.

[27] Jawaharlal Nehru, *Autobiography,* p. 197 ('a bitter pill').

[28] Ibid., p. 259.

[29] For Gandhi's own conciliatory, though rather patronizing reply, see *Collected Works of Mahatma Gandhi,* Vol. LXV, pp. 298–300.

[30] Subodh Roy, *Unpublished Documents,* pp. 389–91.

[31] *Autobiography,* pp. 361–69, esp., pp. 365–66.

[32] Ibid., p. 367.

[33] For the original resolution and Gandhi's speech, see *Collected Works of Mahatma Gandhi,* Vol. LXV, pp. 370–74. In his *Autobiography,* p. 166, Nehru is right is saying that the resolution did not envisage 'socialism', but perhaps

overstates the disclaimer when he adds: 'a capitalist state could *easily* accept almost everything contained in this resolution' (italics ours).

[34] Cf. Haithcox, *Communism and Nationalism in India: M.N. Roy and Comintern Policy*, pp. 164ff, esp., pp. 225–30.

[35] A fact ignored by critics such as Bhagwan Josh, *Left in India*, p. 169, who forgets that the Communists were facing a degree of persecution unimaginable for any section of the Congress.

[36] Cf. Gautam Chattopadhyay, *Subhas Chandra Bose and Indian Communist Movement*, New Delhi, 1987, p. 10.

[37] Cf. J.P. Haithcox, *Communism and Nationalism in India*, pp. 160–63, 180–84; an account with a distinct bias in favour of Royists who opposed the Communists in order to bring about the second split. For an account from the opposite point of view, see *Previous Splits in the AITUC*, CPI(M) publication, Calcutta, 1970, pp.11–14.

[38] Bhagwan Josh's analysis of the contents of these letters *(Left in India*, pp. 167–74) is heavily one-sided; Haithcox, pp. 207–08, is more balanced.

[39] For the text of Dimitrov's report, see G. Adhikari (ed.), *From Peace Front to People's War*, Bombay, 1944, pp. 142–49. As one can now see, Dimitrov's report represented much more than just 'a new tactical line' which it was held to be at that time.

[40] The full text of this article is printed in CPI(M)'s organ, *The Marxist*, October 1995–March 1996, pp. 53–66.

[41] Bhagwan Josh's criticism of the Communist policy following the Dutt–Bradley theses is characteristic. No success could arise out of 'the policy of building a separate, independent mass CP [Communist Party] and a united front simultaneously' *(Left in India*, p. 101). In other words, suicide by the Communist Party was the only way to further the united front. Josh also ignores the successes which the CPI obtained in 1936 and subsequent years, while pursuing the new 'tactical line' of the United Front.

[42] Cf. E.M.S. Namboodiripad, *How I Became a Communist*, Trivandrum, 1976, pp. 204–06.

[43] For example, 225 members of the AICC voted for the rejection of ministerial office and 487 against.

[44] E.M.S. Namboodiripad, *How I Became a Communist*, pp. 207–10.

[45] Figures from R.P. Dutt, *India Today*, Bombay, 1947, pp. 228, 337.

[46] Cf. B. Josh in *Left in India*, pp. 194–95.

[47] On Congress ministries' labour policy, 'dominated by the fear of Communist infiltration', see Claude Markovits, *Indian Businessmen and Nationalist Politics, 1931–39*, Cambridge, 1985, pp. 175–76.

[48] For the transformation of CSP in Kerala, see E.M.S. Namboodiripad, *The National Question in Kerala*, Bombay, 1952, p. 149.

[49] I share the sense of reserve entertained by Utpal Ghosh, *The Communist Party of India, 1937–47*, Calcutta, 1996, pp. 78–81, towards Bipan Chandra's criticisms of the Communists in *Indian National Movement: the Long-term Dyna-*

mics, Delhi, 1988, for not taking a still more conciliatory stance towards the Congress leadership at this time.

[50] Authoritatively expounded by G. Dimitrov in his report, 'The War and the Working Class', 1939, in G. Adhikari (ed.), *From Peace Front to People's War*, pp. 328–46.

[51] G. Chattopadhyay, *Subhas Chandra Bose and the Indian Communist Movement*, pp. 15–16. It appears from the account in Leonard A. Gordon, *Brothers against the Raj*, New York, 1990, pp. 417-28, that members of the Kriti Kisan Party, 'linked to the CPI', were involved, not Communists directly.

[52] G. Adhikari (ed.), *From Peace Front to People's War*, p. 368.

[53] For a summary of this document, see Utpal Ghosh, *The Communist Party of India and India's Freedom Struggle*, pp. 145–50. This six-month delay was to be much criticized later as a sign of the lack of internationalism in the CPI (Editorial in *Communist*, No. 2, February 1949, p. 63).

[54] A few lines later, he writes: 'Gandhiji's general approach also seemed to ignore important international considerations and appeared to be based on a narrow view of nationalism' (*Discovery of India*, 4th edition, London, 1956, p. 483).

[55] Cf. William L Shirer, *The Rise and Fall of the Third Reich*, New York, 1983, p. 1193: 'By the end of the summer of 1942 Adolf Hitler seemed to be once more on the top of the world.'

[56] *Discovery of India*, pp. 487, 489.

[57] In this the Communists' self-respect offered a sharp contrast to M.N. Roy and his Indian Federation of Labour, established in November 1941, as rival to the Communist-led AITUC: it was revealed in 1944 that the Royist body subsisted on a British government subsidy. See Haithcox, *Communism and Nationalism in India*, p. 297n.

[58] Quoted in Shashi Bairathi, *Communism and Nationalism in India, A Study in Inter-relationship, 1919-47*, Delhi, 1987, pp. 199–200.

[59] Nehru's conversations with the Communist leader Z.A. Ahmad on 28 June (May?) 1945, published in *Secular Democracy*, XXV (3), 1997, p. 19. Subsequently, in September 1945, the Congress formally framed charges against the Communists to which the Party replied at length. (See P.C. Joshi, *Communist Reply to Congress Working Committee's Charges*, 2 Parts, Bombay, December 1945. A summary of both parts was then published in March 1946.) The Communists were expelled from the Congress.

[60] Reprinted in *National Question in India: CPI Documents, 1942–47* (hereafter *National Question*), edited by T.G. Jacob, New Delhi, 1988, pp. 16–28.

[61] Adhikari (ed.), *Documents of the History of CPI* (1928), p. 218.

[62] There are, however, important nationalist Muslim critiques of the Pakistan demand from Tufail Ahmad in later editions of his book, *Musalmanon ka Roshan Mustaqbil* (originally published in 1937), down to the 4th edition (1944), now translated by Ali Ashraf as *Towards a Common Destiny*, New Delhi, 1994. Shaukatullah Ansari published his *Pakistan: the Problem of India* in 1944.

[63] Stalin, *Works*, Vol. VII, p. 141; quoted in Adhikari's report, reprinted in *National Question*, p. 54.

[64] Shri Prakash's criticism of Stalin's definition *(Left in India*, pp. 235–37) is also, therefore, off the point. It was not a 'blind allegiance' to this definition which led to the formulation of CPI's sympathetic position on Pakistan; but it was the latter, which, once taken, was sought to be bolstered by a wrong interpretation of Stalin's definition. For a rather restrained criticism of the Party's Pakistan policy during this period, see E.M.S. Namboodiripad, *History of Indian Freedom Struggle*, Calcutta, 1972, p. 39.

[65] See, e.g., *National Question*, p. 98.

[66] *Secular Democracy*, XXV (3), April 1997, p. 22.

[67] *National Question*, p. 117.

[68] Ibid., pp. 126–57.

[69] Ibid., p. 159. P. Sundarayya says of this meeting that 'in fact it revised its [the Central Committee's] reformist policies pursued during the war period" *(Telangana People's Struggle and its Lessons*, Calcutta, 1972, p. 39).

[70] *National Question*, p. 177.

[71] The most detailed narrative of the uprising is set out in Sundarayya's *Telangana People's Struggle and its Lessons.*

[72] *National Question*, p. 190.

[73] *India Today*, Bombay, 1947, pp. 378–91.

[74] Cf. Javed Ashraf in *Secular Democracy*, March 1997, pp. 15–16. Reservations about the Dutt article were expressed in Party Letter No. 4 (May 1946), from which J. Ashraf gives some quotations, ibid., p. 18.

[75] The CC now described Pakistan as the outcome of 'the Muslim bourgeois feudal vested interests, who are seeking for a compromise with imperialism for a share of administration in a divided India' (quoted by Shri Prakash, *Left in India*, p. 254). .

[76] *National Question*, pp. 218–19. The document left no one in doubt that, compared to India, 'a very difficult and dangerous situation' confronted 'the freedom-loving anti-imperialist masses' in Pakistan (ibid., p. 220).

Index

Thakurdas, (Sir) Purushottamdas, 77
Tilak, Bal Gangadhar, 7, 11, 32, 86
Tolstoy, Leo, 5, 24
Tyabji, Abbas, 33

Usmani, Shaukat, 91, 93

Vizaya, 66

Wedgewood-Benn, 67

Zaheer, Sajjad, 100
Zedong, Mao, 86